To dear Gloria
(some bedtime reading)
with my best wishes

Kitty

SOCIAL WORK AND INTEGRATION
IN IMMIGRANT COMMUNITIES

Social Work and Integration in Immigrant Communities

Framing the Field

KATHLEEN VALTONEN
University of Helsinki, Finland

ASHGATE

Published by
Ashgate Publishing Limited
Wey Court East
Union Road
Farnham
Surrey, GU9 7PT
England

Ashgate Publishing Company
110 Cherry Street
Suite 3-1
Burlington, VT 05401-3818
USA

www.ashgate.com

British Library Cataloguing in Publication Data
A catalogue record for this book is available from the British Library.

The Library of Congress has cataloged the printed edition as follows:
Valtonen, Kathleen, 1944-
  Social work and integration in immigrant communities : framing the field / by Kathleen Valtonen.
     pages cm
  Includes bibliographical references and index.
  ISBN 978-1-4724-5054-8 (hardback) -- ISBN 978-1-4724-5055-5 (ebook) -- ISBN 978-1-4724-5056-2 (epub) 1. Social service. 2. Immigrants--Services for. 3. Social integration. I. Title.
  HV40.V2835 2015
  362.89'91253--dc23

2015021233

ISBN 9781472450548 (hbk)
ISBN 9781472450555 (ebk – PDF)
ISBN 9781472450562 (ebk – ePUB)

Printed in the United Kingdom by Henry Ling Limited, at the Dorset Press, Dorchester, DT1 1HD

Contents

List of Abbreviations

EU	European Union
IOM	International Organization for Migration
MIDA	Migration for Development in Africa
MOST	Management of Social Transformations Programme
MPI	Migration Policy Institute
MIPEX	Migration Integration Policy Index
NASW	National Association of Social Workers
NATO	North Atlantic Treaty Organization
OAU	Organization of African Unity
OED	Oxford English Dictionary
UN	United Nations
UNESCO	United Nations Educational, Scientific and Cultural Organization
UNHCR	United Nations High Commissioner for Refugees
UNRISD	United Nations Research Institute for Social Development

Preface

It is hoped that this book will be a source of useful frames, discourses and discussions for migrant social work practice and research. The intent is to situate migrant social work in the broader discourses and currents of thinking on migration, settlement and integration. Transdisciplinary perspectives are strongly woven into the material, since these are essential for a comprehensive portrayal of social inclusion and exclusion processes which are in the background and foreground of practice with migrants. There is a substantial body of migration and integration research across disciplines, and much of this can contribute to a wider understanding of the context and practice issues that we face in migrant social work. The transdisciplinary material presented here can offer additional insights into the field and stimulate ideas for social work linkages into multidisciplinary research.

The book explores challenge and task areas that arise in this area of practice. The approach to understanding settlement and integration phenomena is largely structural, but the personal and community processes involved in integration comprise a significant part of the work.

Contents of Chapters

Chapter 1 looks at broad migration-related and migration-generating processes. Different types of migration flows are described as well as incorporation policy approaches and dynamics in different societal contexts. The treatment of immigration in the media is also scrutinized. Chapter 2 gives an overview of theories and also explains their evolution. This chapter seeks to capture the long term view on how policies evolve and sometimes fail or prove to be inadequate. Chapter 3 examines migrants' relations to and their place in communities, society and the public and institutional systems of reception. Social resistance and exclusion are discussed as features in the settlement environment.

The theme of Chapter 4 is policy and its discontents. Migrant youth welfare in settlement environments and labour market issues are discussed as areas of priority for policy. Chapter 5 examines settlement practice aspects as well as prevailing culturalization framing and the lens of culture, which can have impact on practice approaches. There is scrutiny of how welfare states, the site of social work practice in many societies, have fared when faced with the challenge of encountering diversity. Chapter 6 engages with equality/inequality issues and oppressive societal relationships. It proposes the public discourse as an integration-promoting activity.

Chapter 7 brings the practice gaze to parenting, socialization, protective factors and resilience. Global care chains and the feminization of migration are more recent phenomena which impact on wellbeing in transnational families. Chapter 8 proposes a model of Interconnectedness in Interactive Systems as a suitable social work approach for addressing risks of peripheralization and exclusion in immigrant groups. The final chapter sets out some areas which would need to be addressed. These relate to policy and strategy, social work practice, work environments, social work education, and research areas.

I would like to acknowledge funding from the Academy of Finland project 'Transnational and Local: The Social Integration of Immigrant Communities', led by Dr. Osten Wahlbeck at the Swedish School of Social Science at the University of Helsinki. I would also like to register my appreciation for having opportunities to collaborate with colleagues at the University of Helsinki, and at the St. Augustine and Cave Hill Campuses of the University of the West Indies.

Kathleen Valtonen

Chapter 1
Perspectives on Contemporary Migration and Social Work

Introduction

Migration holds the potential to be contemporary society's most significant social force for building urgently needed forms of wider human commonalities, cooperation and solidarity. Migrants put us in touch with the ways in which societies have moulded their distinct histories which are now woven into the present. The cultures brought by immigrants represent distinct logics honed in the particular social and physical conditions and contingencies in their places of origin. The encounter with the majority populations in destination or 'receiving' countries involves, as it has through the ages, a multi-faceted, challenging and rewarding effort to work through the terms of co-existence, membership and belonging. Multicultural society is a singular testimony to people's and societies' capacity to develop.

Among the many changes brought about by modern-day immigration is increased ethnocultural diversity, since migrants come from a broader range of countries. In this new phase of change in societies, ethnocultural diversity seems to occupy a prominent place in discourse and to represent a novel challenge for public policy and human service approaches. The migrant integration field offers opportunities for forging new forms of cooperation. This what integration is really about, even when it tends to be understood in receiving societies in terms of ethnic difference, a perspective moulded through processes of the ethnification of majority nationalism' (Gullestad, 2000, p.60).

This first chapter will focus on ways of conceptualizing and understanding broader migration-related processes and phenomena. The chapter presents migration and immigration in relation to forces that have shaped and continue to shape these processes. It sets the context for settlement and integration processes which are impacted upon both by the immigrants themselves in agency roles, and by the receiving societies and its institutions. The themes presented here include types of migration, migration dynamics and policy considerations, mobility options for forced migrants, globalization, and attitudes to migration in receiving societies.

In 2013, according to the UN global migration statistics, 3 per cent of the world's population (232 million international migrants) were living abroad worldwide (UNESCO, 2014). International migration is predicted to continue throughout the twenty-first century at a high level. Labour markets and economies are becoming increasingly interconnected and are encouraging labour mobility. At the same time, in economically developed destination countries the populations are ageing and the native work force base is shrinking (Vogel and Triandafyllidou, 2005). Migration can open access to employment, acquisition of skills and training, as well as improvement of life conditions and life chances. For both the destination and source countries it is a driver of development and growth (UNESCO, 2014).

The global context of international migration is marked by deep socioeconomic inequalities and the associated turmoil of political instability. One of the main causes of migration is growing inequality in incomes and human security between more- and less-developed countries (Castles, 2013). For particular individuals and groups in countries where human rights are abused or endangered, migration constitutes a 'safety valve' in the very literal sense of 'safety', and the only alternative of flight for preserving the human right to life.

Migration is an important facet of globalization and international development. As Castles (2003) points out, the forces that drive migration are complex and embedded deeply in general processes of social transformation. Contemporary migrations should therefore be understood in the context of broader social processes with their own systems of dynamics. These social processes can be grouped under three key principles: 'the importance of migrant agency, the self-sustaining nature of migratory processes once they are started, and the emergence of structural dependence of both emigration and immigration countries' (Castles, 2004, p.222). If the full benefits of migration are to be derived and its challenging aspects adequately addressed, far-sighted policies and interventions will have to be explored and prioritized across the many societies which participate in migration, either in sending, receiving or both categories.

Labour Migration

Unequal and uneven economic development in different countries means that opportunity is concentrated in particular regions, societies or sectors. For people who face the threat of economic marginalization, one of the obvious and very traditional responses is migration, whether domestic, to neighbouring countries or further afield. Migration can be a valuable livelihood strategy for individuals and their families. Younger persons are often better resourced for embarking on migration. Youth advantages include health, fewer family or community ties and responsibilities, and importantly, longer term prospects of reaping benefits from migration. Depending on their socioeconomic situation, families and communities often are supportive in many ways of younger adults' livelihood migration. These circumstances are some of the main catalysts of more recent migration flows from economically peripheral regions to more prosperous centres, and from youthful to ageing societies, where the need for labour replacement has been growing for some time and will continue to do so. However, the reality is that in all too many instances, migration remains a harsh necessity or a last resort involving privation and not infrequently the danger of physical harm (UNRISD, 1994).

Cross-border labour migration might appear to be a less usual or even atypical livelihood strategy. Yet in prior and recent history labour migration has been a commonly accepted way for pursuing livelihood opportunities and welfare for families and individuals (Aguomy, 2009). Gabaccia (2006) states that while most humans at any one period of time have remained sedentary, long-distance, culture-crossing movements have occurred during every era of human history. According to the UNRISD (1994), contemporary movements of people in search of a better life may be proportionally of similar scale to those at certain times in the nineteenth century. Inglis (1996) notes that due to the wide range of countries from which immigrants now migrate, the ethnocultural composition of many societies has been exponentially increasing as a result of the migration movements which commenced in the 1980s. She makes the point that the economic and political events which underlie current movements are different from the previous major waves of international migration in the nineteenth and twentieth centuries which comprised an exodus of voluntary emigrants from Europe to the New World.

In the course of broader historical, sociopolitical and socioeconomic developments, the advent of highly regulated national borders and heightened national sentiment have meant that border-crossing puts most forms of labour migration in a less favourable light. Castles (2013, p.122) states that currently 'Most destination countries favour entry of the highly skilled, but restrict entry of lower-skilled workers, asylum seekers and refugees'. At the same time, international migration and internal mobility are a significant way of addressing growing demographic and economic disparities. When they move, most migrants manage to improve their income, access to education, or personal security, even as they contribute to the welfare of their regions of origin. They might also be exposed to vulnerability as they face the risk of being exploited or subject to discrimination situations (Munz, 2013).

Remaining In Place

The other face of migration – 'remaining in place' – should be included in migration discussions. Non-migration or being sedentary can be a free and optimal choice of individuals. On the other hand, for some in precarious living situations, remaining-in-place can be an involuntary condition caused by individuals' lack of possibilities, resources, or opportunities to seek opportunity or safety elsewhere. Thomas-Hope (2009, xxx) reminds us that

> while globalization in terms of the distribution of the power of capital produces the international and national landscape of labour supply and demand, not all persons or groups are empowered by circumstance to traverse across it in the same directions or with the same degree of facilitation. The selectivity of immigration regulations at the destinations introduces freedoms for particular groups to enter a particular country based upon specific criteria.

Transnational activities, including the flow of remittances across borders, are fuelled in large part by migrants' obligations, responsibilities and familial solidarities with those who are in place in the homeland. Migrants do not cut their ties to the homeland or restrict their life sphere to the settlement country. They often place great importance on maintaining their transnational ties. These also need to be taken into account in policies and programmes that aim at holistic integration approaches. Conventional approaches that treat migration and integration in the light of a permanent settlement mode would need to be broadened to reflect 'new realities of global mobility and connectivity' (Castles, 2013, p.122).

Globalization

Globalization is often perceived as accelerating global interconnectedness and bringing about a fundamental transformation of all aspects of life. Bisley (2007, p.21) states that 'sociological understandings of globalization focus on the way in which the compression of social space is reconfiguring basic human relationships. According to de Beer (2009) globalization can be defined as increasing cross-border interactions, which can be economic, social or political. Individual actors, collective corporate or state actors and many diverse groupings take part in globalized interaction in economic, social or political fields. de Beer (2009) gives the example of international trading companies who interact on all three levels: on the economic level through transactions with other companies and markets; through social interaction when they employ people of diverse cultural backgrounds; and by political linking with local and national bodies and governments.

de Beer (2009) explains how societies open up in different ways to globalizing processes.

Economically countries engage in cross-border economic exchanges which are evidenced in flows of goods, services, and capital. Political openness refers to international political relations with other countries, including bilateral agreements and relations as well as membership of larger organizations such as the UN, EU and NATO, for example. Social openness refers to the flows of information, ideas (culture) and people crossing borders and facilitated by technological developments in electronic communication and the Internet. Migration and travel – the movement of people between different countries is one facet of social openness (de Beer, 2009, pp.107–8)

Migration – in-migration and out-migration – is indeed closely related to the social openness of societies, but a comprehensive frame for migration would recognize the interrelatedness of economic, political and social factors in shaping the characteristics of very diverse migration flows and processes. Migration is an integral part of global processes, and in the long run, probably one of the most socially influential. In one sense migration arises from, and is shaped by economic, political and social processes. In another, nearly all societies are being impacted in different ways by the migration flows.

Delanty (2009, p.1) describes the way that globalization processes have transformed social relations especially in the context of 'the overwhelming interconnectivity of the world'. In his analysis of globalization, Beck (2000) draws attention to how national states are being criss-crossed and undermined by transnational actors. Yet globalization is not yet overcoming the state. Globalization is a current phase of social change, while the state itself has been able to respond to changing circumstances for centuries. Adaptability has been its hallmark and central to its success (Bisley, 2007). State boundaries are very firmly in place, and still constitute a formidable factor in determining the nature and volume of migration flows and the intertwined destinies of those who would cross interstate borders.

Mehdi (2004) states that when viewed from a historical perspective, globalization does not signify the emergence of an economic system that is radically different from the one we now have. As pointed out by Bisley (2007) global linkages between disparate human communities have existed for thousands of years. An extensive economy was established between the eighth and thirteenth centuries by the Islamic caliphate. It extended over conquered lands of North Africa, parts of Europe and the Middle East, and the trading networks of Eastern Africa and Central and Eastern Asia. The 'vital elements of human existence' were being shaped in former periods of history by inter-continental linkages of trade, investment, conquest and exploration' (Bisley, 2007, p.35).

Mehdi (2004, p.12) thus describes globalization as 'a complex, indeterminate process, operating very unevenly in both time and space'. This author reminds us that contemporary processes of globalization create new opportunities but also deepen inequality, with negative consequences such as increased social dysfunction and related unemployment and poverty, as well as 'risks that individuals, countries and entire regions may be excluded from the benefits enjoyed in other parts of the world' (Mehdi, 2004, p.12).

Moussa (2004) draws attention to the fact that accompanying the benefits of globalization (information and technological revolution, expanded work opportunities in fields such as communications and genetic engineering) are specific dangers and challenges for countries of the South. Alongside the 'free flow of capital, commodities and services, restrictions and security regulations imposed upon labour migration have actually increased', this being 'particularly evident in industrialized countries, despite the fact that these very same countries have been keen to attract skilled professionals' (Moussa, 2004, p.7).

For countries of origin one negative consequence of migration in the mid- and long-term is the 'brain drain', the out-migration of skilled professionals. This represents a considerable outflow of human capital to more economically developed regions and countries. The opportunity to employ their experts nationally or regionally is lost once these individuals migrate. The costs of replacing these experts are borne by source countries (Moussa, 2004). More recently policymakers and other stakeholders have raised serious concerns over the substantial investment made by developing countries in educating and training citizens whose human capital is lost to emigration. Destination countries derive great advantage from the inflow of skilled immigrants. Since it is acknowledged that 'restricting the movement of highly skilled people is neither ethical nor effective (and skilled people face serious barriers to their productivity in many developing countries), the search for brain drain remedies has begun to focus on circular migration' (Newland, Agunias and Teerazas, 2008, p.16). Although destination countries are involved to a degree in the effort, the promoters of circular migration of skilled persons are mainly governments of the countries of origin, international organizations, and migrant themselves.

Programmes seek to encourage skilled persons to return on a temporary or even permanent basis to contribute to the development of the countries of origin. Programmes aiming at permanent return of expatriates to countries of origin can offer to facilitate services of recruitment, job placement, transport, and initial employment support. With a more recent focus on temporary return, the MIDA (Migration for Development in Africa) programme of the IOM (International Organization of Migration) works to engage diasporas in capacity building and strengthening of central institutions in the homeland on a consultancy basis.[1]

---

1 See Newland, Aguinas and Terrazus, 2008.

It is not possible to halt or ignore globalization, nor is it possible to opt out of being a part of it. It is driven by developments in technology, communication and transportation, which are independent of the actions of governments (Mehdi, 2004). On the other hand, international migration can have a positive impact on social welfare and economic development. Multilateral dialogue and cooperation can point to ways forward for maximizing the beneficial effects of migration. Above all, 'Policies should promote equal opportunity and safeguard the welfare of sending and receiving countries' (Moussa, 2004, p.8).

Migration Policy Challenges

The complexity of migration processes and flows present a challenge for policymakers and governments trying to balance economic and political interests in receiving societies. Castles (2004) observes that nationalist and racist sentiments in immigration countries make it less difficult to swing public opinion in an anti-immigration direction than to be in support of it. Thus politicians might articulate an anti-immigration stance in public, but simultaneously implement measures or policies which in practice allow more of certain types of immigration in order to facilitate pressing economic or labour market objectives and interests. 'Hidden agendas' are symptomatic of dilemmas arising from conflicting interests. Specific objectives are articulated in policy but are contradicted in practice Castles (2004). Countries manage the contradiction between their needs for low skilled workers and non-acceptance of official labour recruitment policy. The growth of short-term casual employment and sub-contracting even in developed economies of northern Europe has resulted in an expansion of the informal employment sector. This has served to mask the absorption of undocumented migrant workers into labour markets (Castles, 2004).

Caponio (2010, p.169) writes of the role of discretion in policy implementation processes, explaining that the toleration of illegal stays in Italy would not have been possible without 'considerable discretion on the part of local authorities in allowing access to services to all immigrants, including irregular ones. The author cites Colombo and Sciortino (2004) in explaining that when the absence of opportunities for legal entry is combined with a growing demand in the labour market for low-qualified, very flexible workers (in particular in agriculture, care- and domestic work), the consolidation of the so-called 'half-closed/half-open' door' immigration policy is facilitated.

Castles (2004) draws attention to misleadingly declared objectives of states which need to maintain their legitimacy while not admitting to past policy failures. Often policies which ostensibly prohibit undocumented migration might be allowing it in unofficial ways that expose irregular migrants to exploitation. Castles (2004, p.223) proposes that this can be understood as the creation of a transnational working class that is stratified by legal status as well as by ethnicity and skill. The vastly different scales of wealth and power in the evolving global order tell that not all citizens are equal and that:

> some passports are better than others. Such hierarchies may be the basis of a new system of global economic stratification, in which migration – in all its guises – is a key element. In this context, migration control is really about regulating North–South relationships and maintaining inequality (Castles, 2004, p.223).

Dunn (2010, p.4) points out the vast power imbalances that exist in transnational labour movements. To illustrate this, the author draws a comparison between guestworkers and the transnationals who access the contemporary elite labour markets.

Boswell (2007) turns focus to the functional imperatives of the state in the area of migration, and the way responses to societal interests and institutional structure are shaped. The author's argument is that migration policy can be understood best by looking at it from the perspective of the state, and by considering how the state defines its choices and its constraints through the lens of its functional imperatives. The issue is over what tasks the government and the administration must carry out in order to sustain their legitimacy and capacity to govern. States can face a dilemma in the area of migration over how to respond to competing requirements and task areas.

The first and least contested function of the nation-state, according to Boswell (2007) is to provide *internal and international security* for its subjects. Migration policy is treated as one part of this state function, leading, for example, to heightened migration security through tightening control over irregular migration. The second function, relating to accumulation of wealth and management of the economy, is to provide *adequate conditions for business and intervening to correct market failures*. Boswell (2007) states that insofar as the state considers that labour migration is important for wealth accumulation, this could be discretely tolerated or facilitated. When public opinion does not accept or acknowledge migration as having a positive impact, states might refrain from formally advocating liberal migration policy. Triandafyllidou (2010, p.13) observes that there are indications that Southern European governments adopt harsh measures for combating irregular migration yet at the same time do not adopt equally stringent labour market policies, preferring rather to close an eye to informal labour in the shadow economy.

The third function which is critical for state legitimacy is termed *'fairness'*. State legitimacy is invariably strengthened when it can protect 'the privileged rights of its own nationals' also at the cost of excluding 'outsiders from access to finite socioeconomic resources' (Boswell, 2007, p.90). The fourth function, termed *institutional legitimacy*, is the one which has distinct relevance for migration policy. It relates to public confidence that the practices of the state are in conformity with the principles of democracy and liberty. Boswell (2007, p.91) states that this includes 'the rule of law, separation of powers, conformity with the constitution, and respect for civil liberties', which in turn will mean that the state will inevitably be faced with limits on imposing more restrictive immigration control policies, on refugee and asylum policy, and on the rights of long-term residents.[2]

Migration thus impacts on these four conditions for legitimacy in different ways. The central importance of migration in political debates is because it poses key questions on how 'the state is, or is not, fulfilling its ascribed functions' (Boswell, 2007, p.91). When requirements for legitimacy are competing, and in the event that states are unable to fulfil these requirements for legitimacy in a satisfactory manner, they might resort to strategies of 'intentional incoherence of policies through implementing or tolerating de facto immigration' or to 'populist mobilization around concerns about security and/or protectionist conceptions of fairness' (Boswell, 2007, p.96). The last strategy strikes a similar note with what Butler (2008, p.258) refers to as the orchestration of 'dyadic opposition as a way of deflecting critical attention to the operations of power itself'.

An understanding of states' functional imperatives and the conflicting interrelations among these can shed light on many migration scenarios. In stable polities which generally enjoy legitimacy and are characterized by stable legal and policy structures and organs, evident gaps between policy and practice reflect the balancing acts engaged in to maintain legitimacy. To illustrate this, we can take the example of a state which might relax immigration controls and admit refugees as a response to expectations in the international community for responsibility-sharing and solidarity in protecting human rights. This constitutes reinforcement of its fourth function of institutional legitimacy which emphasizes the principle of respect for civil liberties. At the same time, it might not be in a position to ignore the third functional imperative of protecting the privileged rights of its own nationals. Thus it can protect privileged rights of nationals by neglecting to enforce anti-discrimination policies, thereby weakening the ability of foreigners and newcomers to compete in the potentially contentious employment arena.

The state shapes its own formula for preserving its legitimacy. It would be important for settling population groups to understand local dynamics of state stability and legitimacy maintenance in which they often find themselves inadvertent players. Social exclusion in the institutional environments of

---

2 See Hollifield, J. 2004. The Emerging Migration State. *International Migration Review*, 38, 885–912.

settlement societies is a multi-tiered phenomenon. As a profession with social justice as its central mission, social work must be keenly aware of how its practice is positioned and carried out in national politically charged contexts.

Papademetriou (2003) notes that the policy responses to migration of the latter twentieth century are no longer adequate for addressing contemporary migration flows. Three explanations are offered by him for the difficulties facing societies in managing large-scale immigration successfully. The deep and unexpected changes which might accompany immigration are seen as giving rise to instability, and introducing elements of diversity related to migrants' origin and circumstances of arrival such as asylum seeking and irregular routes. The complexity of migration poses many policy challenges such as those of reconciling economic interests that seek access to the global labour pool with other interests in the broader society. Finally the economic and social impacts of migration are unevenly distributed, creating categories of 'winners' and 'losers'. Papademetriou (2003, p.55) emphasizes that 'no policy can simply be transferred from one country to another' and that policies must be 'compatible as much with a people's sense of themselves as with a country's social, economic, labour market and demographic realities'.

Forced Migration

In Crisp's (2003) writing on the global politics of asylum, he states that political persecution, social violence and armed conflict have forced people to flee from their own communities and countries throughout human history. Governments, their armies as well as rebel movements in every corner of the globe have moved people by force in order to achieve their political and military objectives. Crisp (2003, p.75) writes that the people who are most frequently and gravely affected by these forms of involuntary migration are 'the most vulnerable and marginalized members of society: minority groups, stateless people, indigenous populations and others who are excluded from the structures of political power'. Even if they succeed in finding a safe refuge in another country, they might never know when or if it will be possible for them to return safely to their place of origin. The 1951 Convention relating to the Status of Refugees and its 1967 Protocol defines the legal protection category, setting out the main standards of refugee status in use up to the present. According to the Convention, a refugee is someone who:

> owing to a well-founded fear of being persecuted for reasons of race, religion, nationality, membership of a particular social group or political opinion, is outside the country of his nationality, and is unable to, or owing to such fear, is unwilling to avail himself of the protection of that country.

It is recognized increasingly that individuals moving in the context of forced migration make their decision against a backdrop of complex political, economic, social, environmental, ethnocultural or human rights pressures and crises. In migration scenarios of today it is almost impossible to separate political catalysts of migration from economic ones. It is as difficult to make 'categorical distinctions between the political and the economic causes and conditions of migration as it is to make categorical distinctions between proactive and reactive migrants' (Turton, 2003, p.9). Many different combinations of factors and events give rise to instability and life threatening situations and conditions. Lindley (2010) has listed violence, persecution, chronic political uncertainty and lack of the means of livelihood as factors triggering 'forced' migration.

I am drawing here on sources from Turton (2003) to explain how challenges arose from the limitations of the 1951 Convention when it was applied to subsequent events and later population groups needing protection. The definition hinges on two criteria: persecution and 'alienage'. The refugee is an individual who has crossed an international border because of a 'well founded fear of being persecuted' in his/her state of origin (Turton, 2003, p.13).

The Convention and other international treaties were initially meant to protect persons who were fleeing persecution from their own governments subsequent to World War II events. The large refugee outflows caused by conflict relating to political independence movements in the 1960s and 1970s demonstrated the limitations of the protection criteria in the Convention. This led to the shaping of regional instruments – the 1969 OAU Convention and the 1984 Cartagena Declaration for the Central American region – which were based on the earlier definitions but included additionally, as causes for refugee flight, external aggression, occupation, foreign domination or events seriously disturbing public order (the OAU Convention) as well as generalized violence, foreign aggression, internal conflicts, massive violation of human rights or other circumstances which have seriously disturbed public order (Cartagena Declaration) .

By reason of being in a 'refugee like' situation although they have not crossed an international border, the category of the 'internally displaced person' was included as an official group 'of concern' in the international refugee regime. These persons or groups have moved 'because of war, violence and/or human rights violations and are outside the protection of their own governments, even if they remain within its borders' (Turton, 2003, p.13). Since 2006, the UNHCR has taken responsibility for the protection of IDPs in conflict situations (Betts, 2009).

The category of 'asylum seekers' refers to persons who have made a claim for asylum and their cases are pending a refugee determination process. Turton (2003) explains that this category subsequently arose in response to the increasing difficulty of drawing clear distinctions between people who move for political as opposed to those who leave for economic reasons. Political upheaval very seldom takes place without violent conflict, economic distress and human rights abuses. In countries of the North, asylum seekers are often assumed to be economic migrants using the asylum procedure as a way to evade immigration controls. In the early 1980s Western Europe reacted to increased numbers of asylum seekers by tightening visa restrictions, introducing carrier sanctions, safe third country and safe country of origin concepts as well as restricted interpretations of the 1951 Convention (Turton, 2003).

Asylum seekers still managed to reach destinations in ways using new logistics involving networks, new communication technologies as well as people smugglers. The fact that asylum seekers use such mechanisms to make their way to destinations does not mean that asylum seekers not 'genuine'. Turton (2003, p.14) observes that what it does mean is that in practice it has become increasingly difficult to differentiate refugees from economic migrants, even though such a differentiation is seen by governments as an essential condition for effective asylum and immigration policy.

The legal interpretation of persecution does not adequately cover many types of contemporary conditions of acute vulnerability which leave individuals no alternatives but flight in order to preserve life. Environmental disasters, hunger and famine, gross human rights violations, conflict and mass violence affecting civilian populations are examples of life threatening situations in current times. Betts (2013) has developed the concept of 'survival migration' to reflect more accurately the range of contemporary life security threats. Betts (2013) makes a call for addressing human suffering at a policy level through expansion of existing protected categories in order to extend international protection to those who currently fall outside the 1951 Convention frames of protection.

Betts (2009) states that it is not possible to draw a sharp distinction between forced and voluntary migration since volition and coercion occur along a continuum. In practice most migration has elements of coercion as well as volition and is moreover likely to be motivated by a mixture of economic and political factors. Turton (2003, p.9) has also commented on the awkwardness of the term 'forced migrant' and the 'fuzzy boundaries between forced and unforced migration'. He cautions that in attempting to separate categories of migrants along a continuum of choice (free at the one end and completely closed at the other) we are in danger of ignoring the most important quality in migrants and in human beings, which is their agency.

Papademetriou (2003, p.42) states that 'the existing international migration system is organized around ideal constructs that are both dated and disturbingly binary' and further, that these 'dichotomies shed increasingly little light on the reality of today's migration patterns'. He uses the example of states being designated as either 'sending' or 'receiving'. In reality many or even the majority of states are both receiving and sending countries. This is indeed evident in many countries in Africa, which are often thought of as sending countries.

Turton (2003, p.8) notices a strange parallel of forced migration with the global cross-border flows of trade, investment, information and people. In the modern globalized world the difference between the rich and the poor is increasingly evident as a difference between a rich minority who are able to travel freely, and the poor majority who are prepared to take great risks to overcome threats which can range from threats to life and liberty to lack of educational and employment opportunities. Turton (2003, p.8) states that:

> From this point of view, the consideration of forced migration leads us, ultimately, to consider the gap between rich and poor countries, and to the question of how far rich countries are prepared to go to close that gap, by means of development aid, trade reform and, crucially, by the liberalisation of migration policies.

Castles (2004) has stated that the 'North–South divide' is a political and social expression rather than a geographical one. It indicates the divide between the powerful nations of North America, Western Europe, Japan and Oceania, and the poorer countries of Africa, Asia and Latin America. It is not an absolute dividing line since there are exceptions such as socially excluded areas and groups in the North and elite islands of prosperity in the South. The author states that the North–South divide provides a useful general term for portraying the globalization-related growing disparities in income, social conditions, security and human rights. These disparities exert heavy pressure among poor populations to seek improved living conditions, security and more personal freedom through migration.

Castles (2004) points out that since weakness in the economy often signifies weakness of the state, people seek a way out of impoverishment and human rights abuses. Multiple motivations underlie what Castles (2004, p.211) terms the 'migration-asylum nexus' that complicates the distinction between economic migrants and refugees. Castles (2004, p.205) concludes saying that 'Reducing North–South inequality is the real key to effective migration management'.

Forced Migration and Mobility Solutions

Long and Crisp's (2010, p.56) article entitled 'Migration, Mobility and Solutions: An Evolving Perspective' begins:

> There is growing recognition that refugees' mobility is a positive asset that can contribute to their lasting protection

In this section, material from Long and Crisp's (2010) paper on mobility solutions for refugee displacement is presented. The UNHCR is focusing more strongly on 'mobility' as offering a possible solution to refugees' displacement. It recognizes that mobility through regularised labour migration might be able to play an important role in addressing the needs of protracted or residual refugee populations who are unable to access durable solutions to their situation through the three traditional means of repatriation, resettlement or local integration. Refugees are often encamped for lengthy periods in refugee conditions in countries of first asylum where their freedom of movement is severely restricted by host states who await their eventual 'return home'. However, in many cases, repatriation is not feasible even when conflict is past. Fragile states in post-conflict conditions are not in a position to provide returning refugees with sustainable socioeconomic livelihoods or access to meaningful political rights.

In the light of the scarcity of alternatives for sustainable solutions to protracted refugee situations, there has been a marked shift in thinking during the last three years. UNHCR now believes that the means of ensuring their enduring access to meaningful rights and sustainable livelihoods may actually be through protection and enhancement of refugees' mobility. UNHCR's changing attitude to mobility recognizes that forced migrants' return home is frequently neither possible nor desirable. Moreover it is being recognized that a positive and valuable contribution to the de facto protection of refugees, asylum seekers, IDPs and other persons of concern to UNHCR can be made by transnational diasporic community networks.

The onward movements of refugees and asylum seekers, as well as increasing urban self-settlement of refugees signify efforts on their part to take initiative in seeking ways out of the impasse of displacement. Long and Crisp (2010, p.56) explain that:

> mixed migration flows, the onward movements of refugees and asylum seekers, the growth in human smuggling and trafficking operations, and the increasing urban self-settlement of refugees – are all symptomatic of a serious imbalance between international responses to forced displacement and the socio-economic protection needs of those who are displaced.

Furthermore these protection gaps are not likely to be bridged by attempts at more effective population containment. More effective protection of forced migrants' rights to move freely presents itself as a workable alternative strategy which will be in keeping with the initiatives being already made by persons in protection categories.

Durable solutions for refugees must involve the regaining of meaningful citizenship. Protecting mobility is also regarded as an important part of combating the human rights violations that frequently occur in conjunction with irregular or secondary movements from the first country of asylum, which is often undertaken in search of effective protection. As Long and Crisp (2010, p.57) explain:

> People with protection needs will move – and should be able to move – in order to find effective protection. This principle is central to the very concept of the international refugee regime. This helps to explain why UNHCR has become increasingly interested since 2006 in the possibilities offered by promoting regularised labour migration as a solution to refugee exile, particularly in terms of meeting socio-economic needs.

In adopting mobility as a potential tool of protection, the UNHCR is taking a rights-based approach to displacement, acknowledging that it is not their physical exile (which is only symptomatic of the loss of such rights), but rather refugees' inability to access their human rights which should be the focus of international protection efforts. Meanwhile states do not cease impeding the movement of both refugees and migrants across international borders.

UNHCR is also exploring mobility options through the use of regularised international labour migration channels. It is proposed that those refugees who are in situations where none of the conventional durable solutions are feasible, could perhaps be admitted to the migrant worker and immigration programmes maintained by states that are unable to meet their own labour market needs. UNHCR notes that many of these programmes also offer opportunities for long-term residence and naturalization, and thus hold the prospect of a durable solution as well as an interim one. Yet the real challenge in the coming years – for researchers, UNHCR and refugees themselves – will be how to bring reluctant states to accept the idea that protecting the mobility of refugees might be a way towards solving the twenty-first century displacement crises more effectively than insisting on return 'home'.

Circular Migration

Circular migration has a long history. At present, international circular migration occurs on a much larger scale than before since distances have been telescoped by modern transport and technological developments in communication. Newland, Agunias and Terrazas (2008, p.1) describe circular migration as a 'continuing, long-term, and fluid pattern of international mobility of people among countries that occupy what is now increasingly recognized as a single economic space'. They state that at its best, circular migration will increase the likelihood that both countries of origin and destination will reap gains from international mobility.

Hugo (2013) states that in order for circular migration to be an effective catalyst for national development in source countries, systems of circularity must be properly managed and well-governed. The author emphasizes that the migration policies and programme in destination countries should be designed to be development-friendly, while countries of origin should make sure that the expertise and capital which migrants bring back should be put to good use. Most importantly, cooperation between destination and source countries would be needed for shaping effective systems that work for the benefit of countries of destination, origin and for the migrants.

Circular patterns of migration fall into several categories such as seasonal work in agriculture, non-seasonal low-wage labour and the mobility of professionals, academics and transnational entrepreneurs. Some governments consider temporary migration as a way to meet their labour market needs without incurring the social and fiscal costs of incorporating newcomers on a permanent basis. However, some circular migrants do plan to, and eventually become settled permanently in the destination country (Newland, Agunias and Terrazas, 2008). Many migrants nonetheless prefer to travel on a circular basis since they are able to earn in high income societies but spend their income in low cost countries of origin, thereby maximizing in a very significant way, the purchasing power of their earnings. An example of this is found in Caribbean circular migration. Seasonal workers from Trinidad, who travelled annually to Canada under the Farm Programme, were able to invest in homes or small businesses in the home country after they had accumulated earnings. Circular migration proved for them to be a stable source of income since the programme was integrated into the government labour market system. Hugo (2013) observes that circular migrants often prefer to be based in their homeland in order to retain their traditional ways, language and other links. They might also prefer their families to do the same.

The governments of countries of origin are often very positive about their nationals' accessing the labour markets of more economically developed countries. Remittances sent back to families make a lot of difference to households and there is the expectation that if human capital is acquired in the destination country it is likely to contribute to development processes in the homeland (Newland, Agunias and Terrazaz, 2008). The employment opportunities are usually very limited in youthful countries and much societal pressure can be alleviated if nationals find work abroad. Thomas-Hope (1999) noted the risk of dependency on migration for livelihoods as well as a possible reduction in corresponding efforts of circular migrants to be active in the local labour market.

Hugo (2013) states that circular patterns of migration can reduce the risks of losing human capital to brain drain. On the other hand, states which prefer temporary employees are often seeking less-skilled and less-educated migrants. However, in the larger context of human resources we can see that in circular migration, human resources of migrants will only be unavailable during the periods of absence the homeland. According to Wahlbeck (2015) when a transnational social space becomes well established, it will stimulate return and circular migration to the country of origin. This will in turn give rise to new migration patterns. New actors will become involved in the migration dynamics between the countries in question, and such movements will persist over succeeding generations evolving into newer patterns in migration flows in the area.

Undocumented and Irregular Migration

According to Triandafyllidou (2010) the term 'irregular migration' is gradually replacing the previous designation 'illegal migration'. 'Irregular migration' refers to a form of migration that is 'not regular' or 'unlawful' because of its violation of migration rules without necessarily being strictly 'illegal' or 'criminal'. 'Irregular migrants' might also refer to persons whose residence is not registered officially, even when they are in possession of papers which may be presented to employers. The author states that the other term 'undocumented migrant' is used with the implicit meaning of a migrant who does not possess the required residence papers. However the terms are often used synonymously.

Human Smuggling and Trafficking

The definition of human smuggling in legal-political and social scientific communities reads: 'Smuggling of migrants is the procurement, in order to obtain, directly or indirectly, a financial or other material benefit, of the illegal entry of a person into a State Party of which the person is not a national or a permanent resident (UN, 2000a). Human smuggling is differentiated from the 'trafficking of humans' which is defined as 'the recruitment, transportation, transfer, harbouring or receipt of persons … for the purpose of exploitation (UN, 2000b). 'Trafficking' means the exploitation of migrants in the receiving country, whether it happens through prostitution or through forms of exploitative work. Potocky (2010, p.373) writes as follows:

> Human trafficking has been described as modern-day slavery. Its victims are exploited for labor, including commercial sex. To control their victims, traffickers use force, fraud, or coercion, including techniques such as confinement,

beatings, rape, confiscation of documents, debt bondage, false offers of employment, and threats of harm to the victim or the victim's family. Positions in which victims are enslaved include field labor; prostitution, exotic dancing, and pornography; domestic servitude; servile marriage; factory labor and hotel and restaurant labor.

Illegal and irregular migration can be independently organized by international migrants themselves. However, human smuggling plays a central role in facilitating irregular migration. It is moreover clandestine activity that is difficult to study. Sources of information come from interviews with smuggled people, reports of policy investigations and court records. Illegal migration arises out of the disproportionate relation between global migration intentions and actual opportunities for legal immigration. Illegal immigration takes many different forms which depend on existing legal regulations, policing, border regimes, reactions of smugglers and migrants toward these conditions, existing transnational networks among migrants and the physical characteristics of the border areas (IMISCOE, 2007).

Smuggled persons have migration motives that are similar to those of other migrants: to improve one's life, to join family members or to escape from persecution. Human smuggling arises out of the existence of borders, and because border-crossing is possible only under certain defined legal conditions. The motivation for global migration far exceeds the given legal possibilities. At the same time, states' ability to control migration is limited. Against the broader policy context, few migration policies fail completely, but all policy objectives are hardly ever achieved. Moreover there are often unintended consequences of policies.

Unattended root causes are an important factor behind policy failure or policy inadequacy for controlling the targeted migration flows which are seen as problematic. Castles (2004) sees policy to control migration as very liable to fail because the cause of both economic and forced migration remain unaddressed. Moreover as long as migration control is based on narrow national logic against the backdrop of global inequality, it will be weak and undermined. The political fields and twists of policy formation in societies are also significant impacting factors in migration scenarios. As Castles (2004, p.871) notes, 'migration processes are of a long-term nature, while the policy cycle is essentially short-term and often determined by the length of electoral periods'.

Immigration in the Media

Kaufman (2014) reminds us that periods of high immigration in any society have invariably aroused some waves of anti-immigration sentiment. If change is rapid and immigration is considered to be increasing ethnocultural difference, the majority generally responds with a politics of immigration. He urges policy-makers to be mindful of history and to adopt a long view that looks at the politics of immigration from many angles. Kaufman (2014, p.267) comments that 'Ethnic change is historically associated with calls for immigration restriction and a general mood of defensive ethnic nationalism'.

Duffy (2014) makes the observation that immigration is a standard favourite in opinion polls. It carries the drawback that many important and subtle facets of the phenomenon are in practice obscured because of the volume and type of questions asked in these surveys. Dufy (2014, p.265) comments that 'there is more nuance in political views than is often portrayed', but it is difficult for politicians to communicate these, since articulation of a more nuanced stance is likely to be interpreted as not taking the issue seriously enough. Thus it is very difficult to conduct a conversation that does not become one-dimensional, as a result of which concerns and misperceptions are deepened. Duffy (2014, p.265) noticed that, ironically, in some senses, 'immigration has been a strangely unifying issue, as even those at the more sympathetic end of the spectrum often agree it has not been treated seriously enough'. Using Britain as one example, Saggar (2003, p.178) states that when anti-immigrant political sentiment is a common theme in public opinion and electoral contests, it finds its niche in modern national politics. This has given rise to the 'race card' thesis by which public attitudes against further immigration are viewed and taken for granted as a semi-permanent characteristic of the political landscape.

Describing populist parties Lloyd (2003, p.89) states that:

> they base their claim for support on having a direct, relationship with their base, and on opposing the political and other establishments of their countries on the grounds that they are remote from (or, at an extreme, have betrayed) 'the people' – and instead favour other peoples – whether immigrants, the bureaucrats in Brussels, Jews, Muslims or Americans.

According to Lloyd (2003), characteristic of populist parties is that they are used to success that is based on providing simple and easily understood answers in largely single-issue campaigns. To 'the compromises and zig-zags of democratic government', they tend to react badly (Lloyd, 2003, p.89).

Terminology

The terminology in the migration field is nuanced, making it possible to use a range of terms which reflect subtle differences in conceptualization of phenomena. In this text, 'immigrants' and 'migrants' are used almost interchangeably although 'immigrants' can carry stronger connotations of settlement while 'migrants' refer to a larger category of those who have moved.

'Refugees' is used in text which treats with this particular grouping and their circumstances. Otherwise, generally in the text, for the sake of convenience, they are not differentiated from the main categories of 'migrants' and 'immigrants' which whom they share much commonality in settlement and integration.

The term 'societal' is used to refer to the institutional as well as the 'public' (as opposed to 'private') spheres of social life. 'Societal' includes both formal and informal planes.

Social work with migrants, migrant social work, integration work or integration social work, as well as settlement work, all refer to professional social work practice with persons of immigrant or refugee background. In writing the text, I tried to weigh each term by its 'usability'. It could be that 'migrant social work' would reflect the field in a more generic way than the others. It might therefore be more useful in conveying the broader concept of practice with the range of migration actors.

Chapter 2
Theories and Frames for Understanding Migrant Incorporation: Past and Current Perspectives

Incorporation Frameworks

This chapter presents an overview of integration models and their development. Earlier discourses relating to the current context of integration are also presented. Integration models evolve in response to changes in migration flows and to developments and events in receiving countries. Models and theories are reflected to varying degrees in national policies and come to influence the ways in which immigration and integration are regarded among the citizenry of receiving societies. There is a very substantial body of discourse, research and literature that has been developed in different disciplinary areas.

Assimilation

Assimilation is the well known and often contested earlier model of immigrant incorporation which assumed that immigrants would need to melt into the main population as a prerequisite for becoming part of the new society. Adjustments of institutions or majority society practices to accommodate new groups was not given prominence since the assimilatory process of immigrant incorporation was considered to be a one way process with the onus of adjustment placed on migrants. The migrations from Europe to the United States in the early decades of twentieth century were largely the focus of American researchers at that time, and they developed the assimilation model to apply to their national experience of immigrations. This perception of a linear one-way incorporation process seems nonetheless to linger on in immigrant receiving societies, especially, but not only, in those with stronger ideas of national homogeneity.

In later decades of the twentieth century distinctly different migration patterns evolved, bringing migrants from countries which had formerly not generated sizeable emigrant flows. The reasons for this were varied. The 'push' and 'pull' factors affecting migration patterns had changed as societies of origin and destination underwent changes in socioeconomic and political conditions. For example, industrial development in Germany attracted large numbers of labour migrants from Turkey. Migrants from the West Indies left their countries and found ready employment in the transport and health services in Britain, following emerging migration paths linking former colonies with the 'mother country'. Such streams gave rise to chain migration of relatives and others who followed in the wake of those who had 'paved the way' and could assist later migrants to settle and make lives in new societies. Much of the migration taking place in the latter decades of the twentieth century can be seen as movement from less economically developed source countries to more economically developed centres. In contemporary language, it was already migration movement from the global 'South' to developed centres in the 'North'.

Greater variance in national and ethnocultural backgrounds of migrant cohorts transformed immigration scenarios in destination countries into the diversity with which we are today familiar. Policy and programme initiatives were taken formally through the institutions in major receiving societies with a view to organizing settlement activity and processes. In societal contexts with more loosely organized or residual-type welfare structures, newcomer incorporation took place informally and very often through the facilitation of organized responses in civil society bodies. Present day modes of immigrant reception continue to be based on varying configurations of responsibility-sharing among state and civil society sectors, which is also sometimes supplemented by market mechanisms. States' legislative, policy, programme and action responses to immigration are influenced greatly by economic and political conditions in settlement societies, as well as the prevailing social and cultural dispositions in the society towards immigration and its perceived repercussions.

The countries in Europe largely adopted an integration approach either explicitly or implicitly, since the assimilation model was not seen to fit readily in the changed reality of increasing ethnocultural and other diversity in new groups. The assimilation model itself was being revisited. Assimilation was recognized as constituting a disrespectful as well as inappropriate approach since it was based on the expectation that individuals and communities would forfeit the cultural distinctiveness of their origins as a condition for becoming part of the receiving society. Assimilation was defined in general terms as 'the decline, and at its endpoint the disappearance, of an ethnic/racial distinction and the cultural and social differences that express it' Alba and Nee (1997, p.863). Critique directed to assimilation contests the principle of 'the total deracination of one's ethnic past' (Kivisto, 2003, p.17). In receiving societies it became obvious that cultural homogeneity or the myth of cultural homogeneity in their own populations could not be held indefinitely as an overriding national characteristic or value.

Integration

Integration is conceptualized as a two-way process taking place through meaningful interaction between migrants and the settlement society. It will entail change in the immigrant's life view and way of living. Correspondingly change should also occur in the institutional fabric of society as it accommodates to new groups in its mainstream (Rudiger and Spencer, 2003). Integration is depicted as a process of becoming embedded socially into interpersonal and associational networks, and systemically into wider economic or political systems (Lacroix, 2013). Traditionally migrants' ability to participate in the labour market and their formal citizenship have been given central focus, with cultural preferences and social interaction seen as an area open to personal choice Erdal and Oeppen (2013). Thus we see integration conceptualized as a process taking place along two dimensions. Under structural or institutional integration can be subsumed education, employment, and, in general, the economic, civic and political spheres. The sociocultural aspect of integration embraces social, community and cultural activity, and interaction (Kallen, 1995).

Integration is synonymous with 'participation' or 'taking part'. According to the definition currently in use in the EU, integration is understood as migrants' ability to participate fully in the economic, political, cultural and civic life of the society. Integration as 'participation' has connotations of action rather than status, and of migrants as actors and agents in role-bearing categories. It signifies the ability of migrants to take an active and meaningful part in the life of the society.

For migrants the level of access to formal and informal institutions and the calibre of equity-promoting mechanisms have an indisputable effect on integration. Furthermore integration is a relationship with society that includes the important dimension of contribution, which is for multiple reasons one of the most solid links to the surrounding community and society. This aspect is frequently overlooked in studies. The literature on migrant employment and unemployment rarely elaborates the significance of migrant employment as a societal contribution that can solidify minority-majority relations and boost solidarity-based cross-group linkages in the surrounding society. This is discussed further in Chapter 3.

'Incorporation' has managed to retain a neutral status in the terminology used for settlement processes. 'Integration' has shed its former negative connotation associated with unwanted imposition of uniformity (UNRISD, 1994). It functions as a generally accepted term to describe the process migrants go through as they seek to settle and become part of the society, providing a useful frame for portraying basic processes taking place at structural and individual levels. Compared with incorporation, integration is more loaded, implying that policy and programmes are put into place by government and/or other bodies, to facilitate immigrant participation in the different spheres of settlement society. Iosifides et al. (2007) notes that efforts are usually made in every receiving country even if the formal mechanisms might not be so prominent.

Integration processes are associated with different styles of incorporation such as participatory, inclusionary and multicultural. In the discourse, assimilation and integration can be seen to take on different emphases. While assimilation includes some ongoing discussion of sociocultural and psychosocial adaptation processes, integration puts institutional and structural processes to the fore. Nonetheless, in practice, there is much that is common in the different incorporation models. Different national approaches can be seen to contain similar policy and programme elements which feature in particular configurations, sequences and mutations dictated by prevailing cultural, economic and politic contexts. While integration has been an official approach to migrant incorporation in many countries especially in Europe, this is often accompanied by articulated multicultural principles which capture more recent aspects of cultural diversity.

Integration can be viewed along a continuum of immigrant experience. At the weaker pole, it refers to participation in less secure jobs, a more tenuous life chance outlook, and eventually much lower earnings-related social security entitlements. Weak integration can have long term effects which can carry over to the next generation. It is useful at this point to look at the affinity between 'immigrant integration' and the more general term of 'social integration' which is a broad inclusionary goal, implying equal opportunities and rights for all human beings. In many societies, and especially in economically developing societies, 'social integration' places strong emphasis on the improvement of citizens' 'life chances'. Nevertheless while settlement countries of the North are generally more developed economically, it would be critical not to lose the focus on life chances. Even though safety nets and social welfare systems are organized to avert extreme material vulnerability of citizens, life chances is still a most salient concept. It reminds us of measures to combat the thinness of formal equality, and the imperative of overcoming sociocultural and socioeconomic gaps between the mainstream and the periphery if genuine access to opportunities is to be realized for minority groups.

Wieviorka's (2011) scrutinizes integration in a critical light. He points out that while the idea of integration is basically open and flexible, it is at present in deep crisis by reason of the distance separating the possibilities of integration and the reality experienced by many to whom it is proposed or imposed. Integration discourse risks becoming incantatory should societies not offer the possibilities of making it a reality.

Scholten (2011) observes that immigrant integration models reduce the complexity of migration phenomena into ideal typologies, which in turn restrict our understanding of integration policy. Scholten's (2011) point gives a starting point for scrutinizing policy and policy implementation. I argue here that there is a grave risk that the focus, intent and spirit of policies might take a meandering turn in their journey toward implementation. Policies are converted into regulations, rules and further sub-categories which might be based on implicit understandings developed from local precedents on the ground. Integration and settlement programmes are impacted by different stages and levels of actor groups in the implementation process. When the outcomes of integration policy are not satisfactory, policy implementation processes as well as the policy, should be the focus of evaluation.

Classic and Segmented Assimilation

Classic assimilation theory has had a central place in US research on the adaptation processes of its early and later twentieth century immigrants. Assimilation was considered to be a process leading to upward mobility for immigrants and their children, which came to be taken for granted as the end state of assimilation. Succeeding generations would thus achieve higher social and economic status as they grew more culturally and linguistically similar to the American middle class (Zhou, 1997a; 1997b; Xie and Greenman, 2005). Subsequently however the relationship between assimilation and upward mobility began to be questioned.

The adaptation paths of immigrants settling from the 1960s onwards in the US have deviated from this classic assimilation mode. More autonomous dimensions entered incorporation processes which diverged from the assimilative path that guided immigrants to merge into the mainstream society through formal compromise of their own cultural backgrounds. The histories and contemporary experiences of immigrants originating in Latin American, Asian and other countries could be observed to be essentially different from those of earlier twentieth century cohorts (Brown and Bean, 2006). The ways in which individuals' and groups' were adapting to the wider social environment took different forms and were not proceeding in a linear fashion. Moreover 'mainstream' society itself was not a native majority characterized by ethnic, cultural or even social homogeneity. It is a wider issue of debate whether societies have ever been as homogeneous as they were formerly held to be.

Despite the fact that assimilation does not sit well with modern scenarios of diversity, the original model did generate valuable insights into some of the processes of intercultural exchange, which over time and generations, are likely to affect individuals' behaviours, norms and values. Assimilation will retain relevance to succeeding models of immigrant adaptation because the model takes into account the psychosocial dimensions of acculturation and enculturation processes that take place at the personal level. The 'segmented assimilation' model described below also has high significance for contemporary phenomena of alienation and exclusion among youth of succeeding generations in receiving countries in Europe.

Portes and Zhou (1993) introduced the Segmented Assimilation theory in which they proposed that immigrant groups could take varying assimilatory paths into an American society of greatly increased ethnocultural diversity. Incorporation or adaptation need not be toward a majority population entity because a wider range of established population groups and communities provided alternatives. At the same time, social stratification, socioeconomic segmentation and inequality was highlighted in studies. Segmented assimilation can be seen as structured in class-specific terms (Kivisto, 2003).

The theory offered a framework for analysing the patterns in which the second generation were becoming incorporated into the social stratification structure existing in the society. It sought to describe alternative adaptation paths and outcomes (Zhou, 1997a; 1997b). Three possible outcomes were set out by Portes and Zhou (1993). The first represents the conventional upward, or linear assimilation whereby individuals take an upwardly mobile route, becoming increasingly acculturated and integrated into the American middle class. The second is acculturation and assimilation into the urban underclass, which is typified by downward social mobility, poverty and the pull of the subculture/s. Moreover an 'underclass'[1] already existed in many of the large cities where immigrants tended to cluster on arrival and settle (Xie and Greenman, 2005). Selective acculturation, the third category, reflected the choice of retaining the culture and values of the ethnocultural community but also becoming economically integrated.[2]

Zhou (1997b, p.69) refers to the 'oppositional culture' that arose among some of the second generation who felt to be excluded from the mainstream and thus experienced frustration over the reality of their own bleak economic circumstances and outlook in the very midst of a culture placing high value on freedom and materialism. Many of the youth responded to such social isolation and the restricted opportunity structure by rebelling against authority and rejecting the conventional goals of achievement and upward mobility. Perlmann and Waldinger (1997, p.912) refer to this phenomenon as 'the second generation revolt'.

Brown and Bean (2006) point out that segmented assimilation studies direct our focus to identifying the contextual, structural, and cultural factors that underlie successful, unsuccessful, and 'negative' assimilation. The studies raised awareness of the importance of uncovering obstacles which constitute possible

---

1   Wilson, W.J., 1987. *The Truly Disadvantaged: The Inner City, the Underclass, and Public Policy*. Chicago, IL: University of Chicago Press.

2   See Portes, A. and Rumbaut, R.G., 2001. *Legacies: The Story of the Immigrant Second Generation*. New York: Russell Sage Foundation.

barriers to the effective adaptation and incorporation of youth at critical stages of their lives.

Some immigrant groups are more susceptible than others to the downward mobility track. Zhou (1997b) pointed out that many of the factors determining individuals' paths could be external to the group, with racial stratification, economic opportunity structure, and spatial segregation being examples. On the other hand, factors which are intrinsic to immigrant individuals and groups include financial and human capital on arrival, family structure, community organization, and cultural patterns of social relations. Zhou (1997b) observed that these two sets of factors exert influence on the life chances of immigrant children both additively and interactively.

The support of the family and the ethnic community can play a vital part in incorporation, provided that these are able to mobilize the resources which could help avert downward assimilation of youth in difficult phases in adaptation and assimilation processes. Social relations in the family or the ethnic community might indeed be able to deflect the trend of negative adaptation even in harsh circumstances. The argument is that ethnicity and culture can function as potential strengths/supports or so-called 'protective factors' against potentially adverse conditions for integration.

The divergent paths of assimilation can be seen from the angle of ethnic identification. In the context of ethnicity and culture, ethnic identification refers to the degree to which individuals view themselves as being involved with an identifiable group. More importantly ethnic identification is reflected in the strength of individuals' investment in (or stake in) the particular culture of the group (Cetrez, 2005). Identification is an individual process, influenced by personal experience, the societal environment and the interactive relation of these.

Ethnic identification was one of the markers in Gordon's seminal model of assimilation. Gordon's (1964) model included the stage of identificational assimilation when immigrants would feel a sense of peoplehood in common with majority society. They would feel bonded with the dominant culture, and in the process, would acquire sentiments and attitudes prevailing in the majority group. Gordon's model has a strong social cohesion thrust and in one sense sees settlement as spontaneously following in the centripetal current of majority society.

The second generation of migrant youth necessarily differ from first generation immigrants. The latter have the choice of retaining or falling back on strong and sustaining frames of reference and reference groups based in their countries of origin. These mechanisms can serve to buffer adverse or difficult experiences encountered in settlement. Migrant youth, on the other hand, must seek their affiliations and a sense of meaningfulness in the actual living environment, and must link into the 'here and now' contexts of their lives.

Overall the theme of identity has occupied a dominant space in incorporation discourse and has evolved with each interpretation of the process. Faas (2010, pp.215–16) observes that 'Europe … has seen an 'avalanche' around the concept of identity'. He states that the focus of identity research in North America has largely been on ethnic and racial identity rather than on political (citizenship) identity. The author stresses the significance of the ethnic/political identity nexus and argues for research and deeper understanding of how such identity processes shape integration. The use of the lens of identity to examine integration processes should be grounded on a strong grasp of the complexities of this phenomenon, of its potential as well as its limitations as an analytic and explanation-generating tool for scrutiny of incorporation processes.

Some migrants might identify themselves ethnoracially in order to facilitate economic achievement. The observation by Waters (1990) shows another facet of identity. This author has observed that ethnic/racial identification might actually become more subjective, and autonomous among later generations. Identity can invoked at will by individuals who feel that they can choose more freely how much they wish to be identified along the ascriptive criteria of race or ethnicity. For these generations, 'ethnicity is not something that influences their lives unless they want it to' (Waters, 1990, p.7).

Multiculturalism

Multiculturalism swings away from assimilation by recognizing the inherent importance of culture and of cultural identity for migrants. Multiculturalism is often described as a way of *managing* diversity in societies. The accommodation of different cultures into the social fabric is in principle underpinned by the formal goal of social inclusion through policies to facilitate full and equal participation by all. Particular policies for addressing issues related to the incorporation of immigrants and immigrant groups can be institutionally located within a formal multiculturalist policy frame. Multiculturalism introduces a diversity oriented dimension into policymaking. It focuses on the need for migrant incorporation-related policy responses and it establishes an institutional space for addressing ethnocultural diversity in populations. Inglis (1996) has pointed out that this purposeful culturally inclusive dimension is lacking from strictly universalist or monocultural approaches. In an interview with Sabarini (2011), Wieviorka states that multiculturalism constitutes a political and institutional proposal to build with ethnocultural differences, and to build in an ethos of democracy. Kivisto and Wahlbeck (2013, pp.2–5) suggest that 'multiculturalism can be viewed in two ways that are reciprocal. It can be seen as a form of claims-making by minority groups and correspondingly, as the way in which the dominant society and its political system will accommodate to and manage diversity'. thus 'rather than forging an expanded societal solidarity by overcoming diversity – as assimilation is generally seen as entailing – multicultural solidarity is achieved through the embrace of difference'.

Multiculturalism has been the subject of much debate since the time of its inception into policy in Canada in the late 1970s. Its subsequent adoption in other countries and its continued resilience in the policy world is largely due to its uniqueness in offering a policy approach and an institutional foundation for recognition of diverse social groupings (Wieviorka, 2014). In Inglis's (1996, p.38) study of the potential of multicultural policies for coping with diversity in Australia, Canada and Sweden, she designates the policy as one that 'accepts the potential, and legitimacy, of ethnic minorities' cultural and social distinctiveness'. Thus the model envisages individual groups' full participation and incorporation into the society without loss of their distinctiveness. It acknowledges formally the legitimacy and need for equality of ethnic groups in the expression of their diverse cultures (Inglis, 1996, p.38). We can say that, in principle, the multiculturalism ideal is to shape a fair policy approach for respecting the cultural integrity of immigrant minorities and to secure their place in settlement society.

Multiculturalism has been accompanied by reservation as to whether the official recognition of group and cultural distinctiveness might invite divisions into the social fabric. Biles and Carroll (2012, p.79) state that, 'Every national government is concerned with establishing the centripetal forces that hold a nation state together. Shared values and national unity form the basis of solidarity in a nation state'. A related question that often arises is over whether individuals' adherence to their own culture and identity would conflict with identification with the wider national polity and society. The policy challenge is to shape and implement multiculturalism as a local and national policy and strategy for building strong bonds of national belonging.

Wieviorka (1998) points out that multiculturalism rests on a political action foundation that supports the right of individuals and groups to maintain a special culture, and simultaneously underpins the society's institutions, the basic law of the state, and the possibility of citizens' full participation in the life of the society in civic, legal and economic spheres. In Wieviorka's (1998) interpretation there is a high potential for mutuality between national unity and multiculturalism.

The Phases of Multiculturalism

Looking back at the earlier phases of multiculturalism gives an idea of how emphases shift in the light of experience with the policy in its operational stages. Canada adopted 'multiculturalism' during the 1970s and 1980s as its strategy for handling increasing ethnocultural diversity in its population. Canadian multiculturalism at this time laid emphasis 'on balancing rights and responsibilities of citizenship, on shared values, and on *connecting across differences'* (Biles, 2012, p.79). It was held to be a celebration of racial, religious and cultural backgrounds. Biles (2012, p.79) states that 'Given Canadian diversity, with the multiplicity of First Nations even at the outset of nationhood, with two major colonizing empires and subsequent immigration from around the globe, the Government of Canada is more practiced at this endeavour than most'. States which later adopted multicultural thrusts moulded the policy to their own national philosophies, needs and contingencies.

Underlying the Canadian multicultural policy was what was dubbed 'the multicultural assumption' by Berry, Kalin and Taylor (1977). It was held that strong ethnic groups give their members confidence in their own identity, which in turn would foster respect for the identities of others and a willingness to share with them. This would comprise a basis for building positive and constructive relations between groups of distinctly different backgrounds.

Multiculturalism in Canada was strongly criticized for side-stepping serious issues of inequality in economic and political power distribution across ethnic groups. The official strategy was considered by many as one that comprised on non-threatening cultural demands in order to assuage the tougher demands from immigrant groups for equal economic, political and social opportunities. Multiculturalism in Canada then adopted an anti-racism thrust that was implemented through anti-discrimination measures in employment, housing and schooling. At the same time programmes were mounted for the promotion of tolerance of ethnic and racial diversity and respect for difference (Kallen, 1995).

In her study of multiculturalism in Australia, Canada, Sweden Inglis (1996) noted increased legislative and administrative action to target institutional and individual racism. In these countries, priority was given also to community relations and education issues. Inglis (1996) observed that the shift of focus from cultural maintenance to issues of equality and the removal of disadvantage was significant across the countries despite the fact that their specific policy initiatives and programs varied with the national context. Inglis (1996) states that the central emphasis in multiculturalism is on promoting equality in all spheres, while enabling the exercise of different cultural practices.

Multiculturalism can be understood as involving the recognition of minority group rights and the promotion of positive relations between and among ethnocultural, majority and other population groups. This is realized through the extension of formal and substantive citizenship rights in the economic, civil and political spheres. Equal opportunity and anti-discrimination instruments (legislative, policy and programme) undergird implementation on the ground. Similarly in the context of 'integration', Wieviorka (2011) emphasized that neglect of integration barriers such as racism, discrimination, social injustice, exclusion, and an extreme precariousness, will in effect defeat the purpose of policy.

In his work on multiculturalism Wieviorka (1998) places like emphasis on substantive equality dimensions. Since incorporation comprises several key dimensions which cannot in practice be separated, a multiculturalist policy should therefore be a comprehensive rather than a selective policy. In focusing on both social and cultural issues, multicultural policy responses should address social exclusion and social inequality along with cultural recognition. At the same time Wieviorka (1998) sees potential in multiculturalism in that it can also be expected to play a positive role in the economic development of the society in which it is organized.

Wieviorka (1998) makes an important observation relating in particular to the social dimension of multiculturalism. This author states that lack of recognition, self-esteem and respect present difficulties far less frequently for well-off or socially mixed groups, than for groups who are most deprived. For the latter, it is precisely because they are socially deprived that they experience difficulty in asserting themselves and retaining their cultural integrity and dignity. Should a minority be culturally different but nonetheless actively participating in the economic life of the society, it is less far less likely to incur social rejection than is the case for the culturally different who are excluded or marginalized (Wieviorka, 1998, p.904). Thus, addressing exclusion mechanisms in society are a critical part of multicultural measures if we are not to equate respect for cultures with the management of social difficulties.

Since it is predicated on structural accommodation and institutional efforts to bring the ideas to fruition, multiculturalism, like integration, calls for state resources and intervention for policy formulation and implementation. Ideally the multicultural model brings in actors from non-state sectors in civil society and the private organizational sector (Inglis, 1996, p.53). Material support from the state for realizing multicultural aims is not a given since resources might not be readily available. Immigrant receiving countries undergo socioeconomic cycles, and have varying levels of infrastructure which could be mobilized to support multicultural initiatives. When in-migration follows a pattern or can take place in a planned fashion, programme responses can be prepared. In countries such as the southern European states which now experience unprecedented arrivals of boat refugees, the existing formal infrastructure is stretched. Refugee situations give rise to the need for extraordinary measures, policy, service and human responses.

Reviews of models for immigrant incorporation are always moderated by the fact that societies and cultures are not static phenomena. Societies themselves are increasingly affected by migration. Demographic change occurs as young migrant cohorts of working age 'renew' the work force and as ethnocultural diversity increases. As ethnocultural diversity grows in receiving societies, adaptation and integration processes will take place in a social environment of expanding sociocultural variation and 'choice'. Cultures on the other hand are sensitive to context, time, contingencies and the social settings in which they are practised. Wieviorka (1998, p.881) says 'Cultural differences are not only reproduced, they are in the constant process of being produced which means that fragmentation and recomposition are a permanent probability'. When examining how cultural diversity is conceptualized in relation to the society and how it is managed, we are dealing with dynamic phenomena. Changes in the demographic base represent only one aspect of how the encounter with new groups affects the society.

Similar to other collectivities, ethnocultural collectivities feature much intra-group difference and variance. Individuals share a background in the same cultural or national context, but are 'unique' persons with their own experience, ideas, preferences, capacities, and value priorities. Groups feature a cross section of diversity among their members. Correspondingly we can expect to discover lines of commonality and mutuality that cut across cultural and ethnic lines.

A multicultural approach recognizes that plurality and diversity exist not only between but within groups and communities. Rudiger and Spencer (2003) state that multicultural integration policies seek to foster permeability of group borders. These authors state that participation by all groups across social, economic and political spheres will promote continual development and cross-fertilization of cultures and identities, thus working to overcome divisions and segregation. In Chapter 9 horizontal and vertical cross-cutting lines of commonality, mutuality and interdependence are discussed as having a role in promoting cohesion in diverse societies.

In his work on the societal dynamics of ethnicity in America, Higham (1984) put forward a concept for a model of pluralistic integration in society. Society would uphold a common culture which would be accessible to all members. At the same time, it would support ethnic minorities in retaining and developing their cultural integrity. This integration approach builds on the idea of ethnic nuclei and ethnic group boundaries. Ethnic boundaries would be permeable. Ethnic nuclei on the other hand would be respected as enduring centres of social action (Higham, 1984, p.244). Thus integration and ethnic cohesiveness would be compatible goals which would be accepted by individuals in differing degrees. Higham (1984) observed that this model was already partially realized in society and he envisaged that the strengthening of ethnic nuclei could in future diminish the significance of maintaining ethnic boundaries in the population.

Higham's (1984) work contributes an interesting version of pluralistic integration that reaches the core of current multicultural debate. Ethnic nuclei and their action initiatives are very observable phenomena in migrant communities. Although the author's frame was developed several decades ago, the concept of ethnic nuclei has contemporary significance and can contribute to the understanding of and respect for the positive potential of ethnicity dynamics.

Parekh's Multiculturalism

This section sets out an analysis of multiculturalism by Bikhu Parekh (2010). It pulls together in the discussion strands of multiculturalism related-theories and discourses which are otherwise often treated separately in discipline-based debates. The author builds into his analysis, the role of values, principles and qualitative dimensions which place social belonging and justice into the centre of this discourse.

Parekh (2010) notes that the appeal of multiculturalism has led to its adoption in different societies and in many differing political contexts. However this has often taken place in an unplanned fashion and without clear understandings of its underlying principles and philosophy. Parekh argues that multiculturalism is a way of viewing human life, and is based on three central insights and on the interplay of these. These three complementary insights are the cultural embeddedness of human beings, the inescapability and desirability of cultural plurality, and the plural and multicultural nature of each culture.

The cultural embeddedness of human beings

While deeply shaped by their cultures and apt to view the world from within it, individuals are nonetheless able to think and to evaluate their culture's values and systems of thought and meaning critically. Some cultural influences can be overcome but not all. It is also possible that inherited cultures might be uncritically accepted, or they might be revised on reflection. Others might even consciously adopt a culture.

The inescapability and desirability of cultural plurality

Cultures are based on their own systems of meanings and perceptions of the good life. Here Parekh's argument is that the totality of human existence can be grasped only partially by a single culture. A culture needs other cultures to expand its intellectual and moral horizon, broaden its imagination, deepen its own self-understanding and, not least, to ward away the temptation of absolutizing itself. While individuals can live within their cultures, access to others will likely contribute in many ways to their lives. International mobility and interdependence in our current world make it unlikely that a culturally self-contained life is any more a possibility. Parekh points out that all cultures deserve at least some respect on account of the meaning they hold for their members and the creative energies they exhibit.

The plural and multicultural constitution of each culture

Parekh emphasizes the internal plurality in each culture and the dynamics of ongoing discourse between its different strands of thought and traditions. Cultures all bear within themselves dimensions of others which they assimilate and have always assimilated. The identities of cultures are thus inherently plural. Parekh's (2010) multiculturalist perspective derives from the interplay of the three insights described above. His argument for the desirability of cultural plurality is based on the grounds of the limited reach of single cultures to capture the full experience of life.

The nature of unity, commitment, loyalty and belonging

On the perennial question of belonging and unity in multicultural society, Parekh (2010) points out that in diverse societies, common belonging and commitment cannot rest on a foundation of ethnicity or culture. He proposes that a common sense of belonging must be political and based on a shared commitment to the political community. Citizens of all backgrounds are bonded by their mutual commitment and concern for the shared community. This holds regardless of how they personally feel about their fellow-members' lifestyles, view and values.

Parekh (2010) does not see the core commitment to the political community as necessarily involving agreement with common goals, with the common readings of history, with the form that government has taken or with the dominant cultural ethos. The essence of the commitment to the political community is members' commitment to its continuing existence and wellbeing, caring enough for it in their different ways so that the firm intention is not to harm its interests and wellbeing, nor to undermine its integrity. This type of attachment could be termed political loyalty or patriotism.

On the other hand, this still leaves citizens with the choice of exercising critique of government, institutions, policies, values, ethos and prevailing self-understanding in the strongest of terms should they think that these might harm the society's survival and wellbeing. Moreover members' social critique should not be read as disloyalty as long as their basic commitment to the community is not in doubt. According to Parekh (2010) patriotism is not the monopoly of the socialists or conservatives, for example, since those who radically oppose might be just as loyal to their community or even more so.

Transnationalism

Transnationalism emerged over two decades ago as a conceptual frame for understanding and analysing the dynamic networks of transactions, communications and ties which are maintained by migrants between their countries of origin and settlement. The anthropologists Glick-Schiller, Basch and Szanton-Blanc (1992; 1995) were the early proponents of transnationalism which they described as a process through which social fields were being created through the building, maintenance and reinforcement of multiple linkages connecting migrants with their societies of origin. This was contrary to conventional notions which held that migration and settlement implied the waning of links with the homeland, as well as with compatriots, kin or friends who might have migrated to other destination countries.

It has been pointed out that transnationalism represents a new perspective on migration movements rather than a new phenomenon in itself. Transnational life most likely was not recognized as such in the past because we lacked a frame or lens through which to analyse such migration styles and to identify common features recurring across migration phenomena. Smith (2003, p.749) states that 'neither transnational life nor diasporic public spheres are new, but that we are only able to see past examples of them by using the theoretical innovation of a transnational lens'. It is however possible to scrutinize some features in modern transnationalism which were not prominent in past examples of transnational movement.

New technologies in travel and electronic communication facilitate rapid commuting and communication over national borders and great distances. Regardless of whether earlier migrants were motivated to retain personal, cultural, economic or political ties with their homelands, the means to do so were not available at the time. Much of the density and complexity of contemporary immigrant transnational practices and networks comes in the wake of modern innovations in communication and travel (Kivisto, 2001; Portes, 2003).

Kastoryano (2000) states that transnationalism has also been fuelled by expanding world trade and exchange circuits of globalization. This might have led to a greater disposition toward travel and border-crossing. Additionally this author points out that multicultural policies in destination countries accommodate cultural hybridity and multiple identities. Kastoryano (2000) put weight on the affective ties and political convictions that are important factors sustaining transnational fields and networks.

Transnationalism has become a central theme in migration. Research and literature treating with this topic is to be found widely across disciplines. Transnational activity has undergone changes, and can be argued to be on the increase. The transnationalism paradigm recognizes the role of migrants' active connections with their countries and communities of origin as one potentially important facet of settlement and integration. Portes, Guarnizo and Landolt (1999) constructed a working typology of forms of transnational activity. These researchers identified economic, political and sociocultural cross-border transactions. Economic transnationalism referred to the fostering of cross-border contacts by migrants who were engaging in entrepreneurial activity and sought suppliers, capital and markets. Political transnationalism consisted of efforts of homeland-based officials, community leaders or immigrant groups to obtain political influence or power in receiving or sending countries. Sociocultural cross-border activity consists of activity aimed at the reinforcement of a national or ethnocultural identity among the communities living abroad. This includes the organization of cultural events, exchange, information dissemination and other culture promoting activities that could be oriented also to the wider settlement society (Portes, Guarnizo and Landholt, 1999).

Transnationalism, according to Smith and Guarnizo (1998), can be understood as a 'people-led' process that could potentially create new ways for economic and political opportunities arising out of globalization to be used to advantage by people on the ground. These authors predicted that this type of 'transnationalism from below' would be a significant force which would be a balance to nationalistic tendencies and the inward-focused centralizing tendencies of nationalism. Additionally people-led transnationalism could be a challenge to powerful large-scale corporate and interrgovernmental transnational structures'. Nearly twenty years have passed since the publication of Smith and Guarnizo's (1998) book on 'transnationalism from below'. The authors' prediction that it would be a force to reduce the inward-focused centralizing tendencies of nationalism has been proven to be true in the sense that migrants' ties and identification with their homelands are sustained in tangible and intangible ways and have assumed critical importance in the life of many immigrants who are settled and established in settlement countries. The fact that settlement and integration take on a transnational dimension indicates that border permeability exists on the plane of connectedness, if not in the area of border control.

In a more person-based definition, transnationalism has been seen as a coping strategy for migrants who strive to manage their integration into two or more settings (Lacroix, 2013). Transnationalism in this sense does not dissolve borders and territories. Instead it leads to a process whereby political/social/economic discontinuities become appropriated in individuals' quest for legitimacy of in-betweenness (Lacroix, 2009; Smith, 1994). According to this definition we can understand migrants' engagement in transnationalism as a way of meshing relations to two or more social sites or societies into a composite arena of active human relations.

Transnationalism is also a complex human phenomenon. The affective dimensions such as obligations, nostalgia and patriotism are powerful factors in sustaining transnational fields and networks (Dunn, 2005). Smith (2007, p.1096) examined political transnationalism, migrants' dual loyalty and national identity formation 'on both sides of the US-Mexican border'. Since individuals have ties to both settlement society and the homeland, they can experience ambivalence towards life and how political life is conducted in either one, as well as towards the modes of political participation in which they might engage. The author states that 'loyalty' is thus never unalloyed and always contingent. Individuals 'continue to act politically, both 'here' and 'there', and do so with a growing sense of transnational political efficacy' (Smith, 2007, p.1114).

In an ethnographic study of a migration flow linking Ecuador and Italy, Boccagni (2012, p.275) describes the tie between migrant parents and their children in the homeland as 'a relationship that by far exceeds money remittances, in the light of the intimate ties it may be fuelling'. Bukasa's (2010) study of Congolese migrants in South Africa finds that there are constraints involved in the maintaining of transnational ties. Migrants' strong awareness of their role expectations in their communities of origin exerted pressure to be perceived as 'successful' in the new environment. Bukasa (2010) states that migrants seek to foster familial belonging over distance and at the same time to sustain social status. Additionally remittances are seen as a means to avoid social stigmatization and exclusion from social networks. Dorais (2009) has studied Vietnamese transnationalism in Montreal and found that strong family attachments underpin and support the continuity of relationships with kin in other countries.

Transnationalism can be described as the ties and links which migrants sustain with those in the country of origin and in other destination countries. These multi-site cross-border human and social relationships are operationalized through communication, exchanges and transactions, the functions of which include maintenance of affective ties, working collectively toward instrumental ends of an economic, political, civic or sociocultural nature.

In the political arena of transnational activity, networks of transnational advocacy and activism have arisen to give 'voice' to individuals and groups who, on their own, would not be able to muster enough support to be heard in the public sphere. Such networks have been made possible by the development of electronic and internet communication. International activist groups can draw on collective efforts for building a platform to work for social change. Transnational activism can provide a common forum of communication and initiatives for refugees who are concerned with conditions in homelands but are scattered in different continents and settlement locations. Activism can focus on human rights issues and be operationalized through transnational campaigns. It can be seen in the context of global civil society.

Feminist sociologist Mernissi (2000)[3] has drawn attention to how digital communication has dramatically opened the realm of public dialogue to women in Islamic countries. Mernissi (2000) states that public dialogues are a fundamental element of any civilized society because they furnish a distinctive and secure space where violent and discriminatory traditions originating in tribalism can be confronted and eliminated. Law (2003) suggests that transnational cyber publics are creating new political spaces for labour migrants in Asia. The author

---

3 The New Cheherazads: Women and Civil Society in Digital Islam 2000. Text for her word-image exhibition and workshop project at the American University, 15–16 April 2000.

states that the advocacy work of groups is critical to improving the working and living conditions of those who seek employment abroad. By using new mediums and creating new media for speaking about migrants' lives and rights, these groups are creating new ways for imagining and thus for experiencing the work of migrant labour.

Translocal

Researchers have made the point that while transnational activities take place across borders and in different national territories, the transactions, exchanges and circuits are generally grounded at meso- or community level. Waldinger and Fitzgerald (2004) argue that transnationals are not actually nation-to-nation but are village-to-village or family-to-family, and that translocalism may be a stronger concept. The 'translocal' discourse seeks to anchor transnationalism into the specific contexts in which it is practised. Dunn (2010), Smith and Guarnizo (1998) and Wahlbeck (2004) are among the authors who have argued that transnational phenomena are not deterritorialized, as the term 'transnationalism' has led many to believe, but connected to and firmly rooted in specific localities. This argument is moreover in keeping with Smith and Guarnizo's (1998) observation that migrant transnationalism is basically a people-led process. It involves, as Portes (2003) has pointed out, private grass-root actors, or nongovernmental, noncorporate actors from civil society.

Concern has been expressed over the risk of exaggerating mobility in the conceptualization of transnationalism. Dunn (2010) recommends adopting an embodied approach to offset the dangers of exaggerating mobility and footloosedness when using the term. Since 'transnationals are simultaneously mobile and emplaced', a much more complex and realistic picture will emerge if 'the scale of analysis is upon migrants rather than migration flows, and upon transnationals rather than upon transnationalism' (Dunn, 2010, p.1). The concept of transnationalism, on the one hand, can highlight fluidity of cross-border movements, and the emancipating dimension of not being tied to one national territory or to a single local or national opportunity structure. On the other hand, the human dynamics which underlie transnationalism need to be acknowledged in order to gain a more comprehensive understanding of this phenomenon.

Transnational individuals leave one national territory to live in another. In the long term they retain important links to kin, contacts or associates in the homeland. While some become transnationals, others remain in place in the homeland, comprising the vital homeland nodes of transnational practices. Some cross borders in a voluntary fashion while for others the decision is driven by the lack of viable alternatives in the homeland opportunity structure. Furthermore the involuntary immobile might be seen those who lack viable opportunities, would seek opportunity elsewhere, but have not the necessary resources to do this.

The need to ground research on transnationalism is based on the realization that transnationals are emplaced and strongly connected in various ways to the environment of settlement, which in turn influences their transnational practices. Moreover the other parties to transnational activities and synergies are also emplaced in their living spaces or transnational nodes. Transnational actors' lives on the ground anchor and make possible the exercise of transnational practices. As Glick-Schiller, Basch and Szanton-Blanc (1995) explain, transnationals are not sojourners since they settle and become part of the economy and political institutions, localities, and patterns of daily living in the country where they actually reside. 'However, at the very same time, they are engaged elsewhere in the sense that they maintain connections, build institutions, conduct transactions, and influence local and national events in the countries from which they emigrated' (Glick-Schiller, Basch and Szanton-Blanc, 1995, p.48).

Diaspora

The concept of diaspora describes how immigrant identities are formed in relation to real or imagined 'homelands'. It is one form of transnationalism (Wahlbeck and Olsson, 2007). The focus of diaspora studies is on dispersed populations. The concept originally referred to the dispersal of Jews from their historic homeland. In current usage the concept often describes established communities who reside away from their homelands, but share an experience of displacement (Wahlbeck, 2002). Wahlbeck (2002) has proposed that the concept of diaspora can function as a useful tool of analysis in studies of contemporary refugees in countries of settlement. It can shed light on migrants' specific relationships to their societies of settlement and origin, thus bridging the analytical gap between them. Cohen (1997, p.196) points out that diasporas can 'provide an enduring, additional or alternative focus of loyalty and identification to the fealty demanded by the nation-state'. Van Hear's (1998) research has shown that diaspora processes do not follow a single trajectory. They can lead to very different outcomes. Some processes lead to strengthening of the existing diaspora, while others can lead to regrouping or to the unmaking of a diaspora, as in the case of ethnic cleansing.

Migration and Development

Recently there has been international interest in the migration and development link, which brings to the fore the role of migrants as actors in development processes in countries of origin. Migrants' transnational practices are often geared to the meso level of homeland development and lead to migrants' economic and social investments into the infrastructure of their communities of origin. Examples can be found in educational, health and cultural facilities as well as a multiplicity of other programmes to improve local living conditions, life chances, quality of life and security for citizens. Migration and development activity can be understood as a form of civic transnationalism.

Codevelopment

As a rather recent policy initiative, codevelopment recognizes that civic transnationalism activity not only benefits the homeland communities which are targeted, but also offers a unique opportunity to affect migration root causes in sending countries. It opens a way to make a direct input into local human development processes in the sending countries. The cumulative outcome could result in improved life conditions for the local population and the creation of viable life chance alternatives to out-migration. This issue can be scrutinized against the backdrop of the wider question of migration motivation. Economic or labour migration is generally seen as so-called 'voluntary' migration as opposed to 'forced' migration – the classification for persons and groups fleeing life threatening conditions. In reality, as discussed in the preceding chapter, much of labour migration is not purely voluntary, but driven by lack of viable livelihood alternatives at home. Not least, in absence of official safety net or social security systems, labour migration is a way for individuals to address responsibilities for supporting dependents by leaving for places where there is opportunity to earn income.

Ostergaard-Nielsen (2011) states that in Spain the emerging policy field of codevelopment took its cue from heightened international interest in the migration–development nexus. Spain is one of Mediterranean countries which have in recent times become new immigrant 'gateways'. Waters and Jimenez (2005) refer to traditional immigrant gateway cities such as New York. New gateways refer to cities or regions of destination which previously have had no significant history of in-migration. New gateway countries include, for example, Southern European countries (such as Italy and Spain which were formerly countries of emigration) and Finland (which had few non-European immigrants before the 1990s (Alghasi, Eriksen and Ghorashi, 2009).

In Spain local governments began codevelopment programmes as part of local-level strategies for migrant integration. Codevelopment strategies incorporate migrants' interest in the development of their homeland communities and regions. Ostergaard-Nielsen (2011, p.21) states that regional, national and local political actors in Mediterranean countries have 'picked up on international trends encouraging a multi-level public policy that promotes the role of migration and migrants in development of their countries of origin'. Transnational links and practices form part of the receiving countries' initiatives for addressing the root causes of migration.

Spanish codevelopment policies were initially focused on how migration management (return migration) and remittances might improve conditions in the migrant-sending context. Since then codevelopment policies shifted to include migrant integration in the policy focus. Thus, as Ostergaard-Nielsen (2011) states, the type of citizenship which is envisioned for migrants under codevelopment becomes transnational when migrants' transnational interests and engagement are seen as an integral part of their local incorporation. The author observes also that codevelopment policies are less linked to issues of migration management. Its advocates hold that a more long-term focus on migration root causes could well constitute an effective counterweight to the focus on security and control.

The 'integration here, development there' principle central to codevelopment breaks new ground. Conventional national and local debates often focus on narrower models of migrant incorporation into settlement contexts, while ignoring individuals' vital connections with their communities, kin and countries of origin. However 'citizens increasingly live their lives across borders' (Ostergaard-Nielsen, 2011, p.35).

From another angle, it is clear that certain conditions in the receiving society could inhibit migrants' transnational practices. If individuals and their families are unable to attain a reasonably sound footing in the settlement country, they would lack key resources to maintain and develop active cross-border connections, ties or exchanges. This situation can prevail if the receiving environment is harsh from an economic point of view, offering little opportunity for individuals to become gainfully employed. In affluent countries individuals can become marginalized from mainstream channels of opportunity due to overt or covert mechanisms of discrimination or closure. Transnational potential as a human development tool in sending countries will need suitable integration environments in order to be realized.

Methodological Nationalism

The study of transnational communities and migration can help to open up the way we view society and the nation state. The term 'methodological nationalism' is used by Wimmer and Glick-Schiller (2002, p.302) to refer to the widely held 'assumption that the nation/state/society is the natural social and political form of the modern world'. The authors state that it is often taken for granted that societies in general embody cultural homogeneity and that its population groups are internally integrated into a 'nation'. Wimmer and Glick-

Schiller (2002) argue that when a state has come to consider that it represents a stable homogenous national culture, the cross-border movements of migrants then are seen as introducing an anomaly or foreign element into the receiving society. 'The societies of today are viewed as composite entities embodying an economy, a political system/polity, their own very distinct culture and people who belong to this nation' (Wimmer and Glick-Schiller, 2002, p.317).

Dunn (2005) drew on the example of Arab and Muslim-Australians, who perceived themselves as bearing the brunt of new terror laws and police actions, while being deprecated in media and in government rhetoric.[4] Transnationals find that they are caught in a bind when they come to be seen as the despised 'enemies within' or the 'traitors abroad' (Dunn, 2005, p.26). The author suggests that normalization of dual and multiple national loyalties into the transnational paradigm might be a way to address nationalism related sectarianism. Migrants' claims to national belonging and to their evolving ties to the local settlement culture should be recognized, along with acceptance of the 'multi-scalar nature of their identifications beyond the boundaries of proximate community, locality and nation' (Carruthers, 2013, p.214).

The assumption that states are discrete and self-contained 'nations' raises concerns about the incompatibility of migratory and transnational movements with national interests. Migration and transnational practices make it necessary to revisit the idea of impermeable borders, discrete national and cultural entities, bounded societies and indeed societies and communities sufficient in themselves.

---

4   Islamic Council of New South Wales (2004); Klocker and Dunn (2003).

Chapter 3
Immigrants in Society

Immigrants groups represent a microcosm or at least a partial cross section of the society from which they have originated. Diversity is a characteristic of such groups which often feature a mosaic of intra-group distinctions. For statistical or administrative purposes however, they fall into a single 'category'. Social variance, intra-group formations, subgroupings, and marked distinctions in such collectivities have been seen as issues internal to immigrant groupings which are categorized primarily by national origin. Immigrant groups are themselves used to issues of intra-group diversity when faced, for example, with the need to build a consensus base for launching needed community initiatives in settlement. Distinctions in groups include those of political allegiance, socioeconomic status, as well as ethnic, cultural, religious and linguistic variations. The processes of migration and settlement can bring about change in the original patterns of diversity and commonality that were typical of communities in the homeland. A policy example of this is when dispersal is wide in geographical resettlement.

The diversities in immigrant ethnocultural groups did not generally attract much notice in settlement societies where cultural differences between majority and new immigrant groups caused more concern for policy makers and the human service providers. However the range of 'difference' in Muslim population groups in settlement countries has more recently become evident. The occurrence of attacks of violence brought about by extremist groups working under fringe interpretations of Islam, and recently the tragedy of Charlie Hebdo, are a steep challenge for social analysts and policy making. When population groups with immigrant backgrounds have been mainly viewed as integral cultural or cultural/religious entities, the boundaries of the problem are difficult to delineate. Commenting on public reactions of Islamophobia, Waltzer (2015, p.109) points to the failure to make the 'distinction between the historic religion and the zealots of this moment' and to 'acknowledge the towering achievements of Muslim philosophers, poets, and artists over many centuries'.

The shaping of appropriate strategies to address such threats to internal safety and security has become an urgent priority. One fundamental element of policy and intervention responses would be to bring in and involve the wider immigrant community as part of the 'solution'. Community leaders and trusted representatives, including in this case religious representatives, would contribute emic 'insider' viewpoints on the evolution of problems and the likelihood of success in alternative approaches. Inclusion of the community, through its representatives would reinforce the legitimacy base that would be critical for carrying out measures to address this difficult challenge. In the unfortunate face of tragedy, responses highlight the value of cooperation between political and public policymakers and communities.

Communities, Categories and Publics

Immigrant groups are often referred to in terms of 'communities', for example, refugee communities, immigrant communities, and 'community organizations'. Calhoun (1999) claims that the term 'community' in used in a general fashion that masks the distinctions among different types of social groupings. Calhoun distinguishes between three community types as follows: 1. Communities or relational networks – relatively small sized groups which are not constituted by formal political-legal institutions. They are based on informal, direct interpersonal relationships; 2. Categories (cultural and legal) based on assumed cultural similarity or other formal equivalence of persons. These are commonly comprised of large numbers of people with a low density of directly interpersonal ties, and 3. Discursive Publics or groupings of individuals whose purpose it is to engage in discourse and expand their knowledge of the nature of social institutions and states.

In the settlement and integration field, the term 'communities' is very commonly used to refer to larger collectivities of persons of the same ethnocultural background, regardless of whether interpersonal ties exist. The specificity in Calhoun's (1999) typology of community types is useful here in that it helps us to differentiate between the distinct activity forms in informal 'communities' and discursive 'publics'. The former groupings are linked by interpersonal ties and intra-group mutualities in the private life sphere. For immigrants, interpersonal engagement with 'communities' of their choice is without doubt important for quality of life. Communities featuring a membership mix of both majority and minority group individuals are socially linking and potentially supportive structures that can promote settlement and facilitate adaptation across the groups.

Publics are focused outward into the wider social environment, and seek to explore the functional dynamics of social and national institutions and structures. 'Publics' serve as conduits for information, and as collective channels for generating information. New citizens and newer members of the society should be positioned near to or in information flows in order to be aware of developments in society which concern them. An informed pursuit of integration is an invaluable advantage when dealing with challenges and unexpected difficulties that arise in the encounter with institutions and structures in a new social environment.

The activity of publics constitutes engagement at the level of discourse within the public sphere of society. Participation in 'communities' is very different from participation in 'publics'. Calhoun (1999) emphasizes that the idea of the public is crucial to conceptualizing democratic participation. Moreover in settling immigrant groups, publics are a marked feature. The lived experience of individuals who migrate is one of constantly engaging in a reflective way with the surrounding social and institutional environment. Their life circumstances, as well as the task and challenge areas of coping in a new society, make it natural, as it were, for individuals to cluster and engage with each other in appraising, questioning, juxtaposing contradictory phenomena and gaining understanding of the social world with which they interact. Publics of immigrant background explore multicultural and cross-cultural issues which are part of their everyday lives in settlement. In any ethnocultural group, there may be several informal publics that coalesce around specific interests, areas of enquiry and varying ways of thinking and relating to social issues. In qualitative studies of integration field work often includes dialogue and exchange with members of such publics.

These publics are often very low profile because of the extremely weak vertical integration in many settlement societies. Their members are seldom in visible, valuable or prestigious positions in the society. However, it is in these groupings where we would need to look for singular understandings of what is taking place in the settlement and integration experience of the new immigrant minorities. Immigrant publics can be fruitfully involved in policy processes to inform and shape the conditions of integration as part of substantive social citizenship.

Civil Sphere

Civil society can be an elusive concept in its flexible and adaptable interpretations. In his writings on civil society in African contexts, Lewis (2002, p.572) has likened the term to a hatstand, convenient for hanging ideas on politics, organization, citizenship, activism, and self-help. The author identified two distinct traditions in the civil society discourse. The first centres on the organizational arena, comprising nonprofit and voluntary bodies which provide services. The second tradition places emphasis on civil society as a sphere that is distinct from the state, the site of ideologies and social collectivities which can engage in challenging the established order. This facet of civil society is closely related to the 'discursive public' in Calhoun's (1999) typology above, but it can be inclusive of different forms of social action and activities which evolve out of scrutiny of the established order. The traditions in civil society are differentiated for conceptual purposes. In practice these are interrelated.

45

The organizational dimension of civil society has become very familiar as the programme or project implementation mode in social and human development contexts. Organizational civil society actors can also work alongside state social welfare service providers. The matrix of arrangements in which these two providers complement each other depends on how the responsibility for welfare and service provision is shared between state, market and civil society agents. In some welfare systems, civil society bodies can function alongside state agencies and market service providers. In the Nordic welfare state model, the welfare service provision arena is largely the province of the state.

Civil society initiatives have much potential in the settlement and integration field. Unlike the larger state agencies, they can directly integrate citizen and user participation elements into their structures. This is a key element in the building of appropriate service responses that would be 'nearer' to newer citizen and migrant groups. In settlement environments immigrant organizations have come to operate in many different areas, spanning mutual helping and support in integration matters, information dissemination, social outreach, cultural and political pursuits. Some function as interest groups around specific issues. They are generally low threshold sites of participation for individuals interested in contributing their efforts to causes in which they are interested or committed. Such organizations are rooted in immigrant communities and are probably the collectivities in closest proximity to the pulse of integration and settlement processes and demands.

Since there is very seldom a high level of uniformity or conformity across national or ethnocultural groupings, immigrants organizations also cater to diverse interests or needs of their own 'constituencies'. When national or ethnocultural communities are larger they can have greater capacity to respond different needs, interests or issues across the internally diverse community. For example, there might be several linguistic groupings in one ethnocultural category. If this category is sufficiently large there is greater likelihood to have interpreting and social support resources to cater to different sub-groupings. In numerically small groupings, this is not possible. This might be one of the attractions for immigrants to engage in domestic or secondary migration towards cities and larger migrant concentrations.

The potential of immigrant organizations can be developed to constitute a valuable resource in the field of settlement and integration, as can be witnessed in several of the experienced receiving societies such as, for example, the US and Canada. The successful development of the potential of immigrant community organizations is influenced to a large extent by how they are positioned in the institutional fabric of the society, that is, on whether they can be seen as contributing agents and integration stakeholders or simply in service receiving roles in which their compliance with the existing system is uppermost. In particular, this is the situation in societies with tightly organized and comprehensive welfare systems which in one sense, crowd out the unique potential for immigrant agency in integration service provision roles.

Immigrant communities' capacity and characteristics will also affect how organized activity will evolve. Chaskin et al. (2001) propose the key factors of community capacity to be its resources of human capital, social capital and the organizational skills which can be mobilized to address collective problems and improve or maintain the wellbeing of that community. The model is focused at the community level. The resource base of its members is the decisive factor in how community organizations will develop a functional role. Collective activities of many types are carried out through informal social processes and transactions. These can also be operationalized through more systematically organized efforts of involved individuals, organizations, and the social networks linking them to the larger systems of which communities form a part.

Community organization activity is not without its headaches and immigrant organizations are no exceptions. Among the members of immigrant groups are individuals who are highly motivated toward improving the conditions of settling immigrants and the terms of their settlement. Vogel and Triandafyllidou (2005, p.11) observe that 'only a minority of immigrant and native populations will be able and prepared to devote their time to demanding forms of civic activism', yet 'these are very important persons, as they may influence or even shape the integration process of whole communities'. These agents of change are individuals with 'a societal commitment and explicitly pursue objectives aiming at the organization of society, community and economics in a democratic way' (Vogel and Triandafyllidou, 2005, p.11).

Personal experience gives individuals a deep comprehension of the difficulties encountered in integration processes, the risks of negative repercussions and the benefits of appropriate and timely assistance. The common experience among refugees, for example, can be understood through Lewin's (1946, p.34) very early studies in the state of Connecticut, of the dynamics of inter- and intra-group relations among groups including 'representatives of communities, school systems, single schools, minority organizations of a variety of backgrounds and objectives' as well as 'labor and management representatives, departments of the national and state governments, and so on'. Lewin (1946, p.42) observed the processes of development of group relations, described by him as transformation 'from a multitude of unrelated individuals, frequently opposed in their outlook and their interests, into cooperative teams not on the basis of sweetness but on the basis of readiness to face difficulties realistically, to apply honest fact-finding, and. to work together to overcome them'. The author's work is better known by the more familiar term 'interdependence of fate', whereby groups can come into being on a psychological plane, not necessarily on the basis of similarity among members, but when these realize that their fate depends on the fate of the whole group. The members of a grouping thus are linked by a keen recognition of their common predicament. In the present integration context, individuals would recognize common challenges and difficult problem situations encountered in adaptation and settlement. Many are ready to commit to and participate in collective civil society initiatives. Moreover participation in community organizational activity is known to be a rewarding experience, in addition to being a constructive effort.

Collective identity is a concept with relevance to community relations. Melucci (1989) brought prominence to the concept of collective identity through his studies of social movements of the late 1980s. The concept attracted the interest of political process theorists. Collective identity is seen by Melucci (1989) as underpinning internal cohesion and commitment in community groupings. Without it there is a high risk of eventual group fragmentation.

In Chesters and Welsh's (2011) processual definition, collective identity refers to the outcome of work conducted by actors in the collective to generate shared understanding of the issues at stake, the terms under which different actors (individuals, groups or networks) might work together and the types of action required to effect change. This stage of *collective identity work* is often not consciously focused upon although keen awareness of its importance will probably exist among the individuals who are attracted to such collectivities. The key issue is how to create the 'we' feeling and commitment in the group as a platform for further activity.

Attaining collective identity in a group requires the investment of effort. Some commonalities in groupings can contribute in advance to the reinforcement of collective identity. These might include common experience or similar cultural background or identity, for example. However this is distinct from the *work* of collective identity construction that takes place *within* the collectivities or movements (Chesters and Welsh, 2011). Furthermore it would be vital for organized collectivities to understand the nature and functioning dynamics of the social and political systems, as well as the fields of power, in which the problems to be challenged are embedded. Since the context of collective action changes, organizing collectivities should be prepared that correspondingly changes will take place in how their focus of activity is directed, leading possibly to the need for re-negotiating collective identity. Critical is the self-reflexive capacity of actors to situate themselves in the context of action and to adapt their practices accordingly (Chesters and Welsh, 2011; Melucci, 1996).

Immigrant community organizations are often viewed as one of many forms of organizational activity. As mentioned above they can engage in a wide range of activities and very frequently as mutual support networks related to supporting the integration processes in various ways. They can be seen as interest groups. If articulating distinct and controversial claims, they might be seen as engaging in 'contentious politics' in the arena where political claims can be put forward *as part of* democratic processes. Much will also depend on the nature of settlement societies, which vary greatly in their participatory levels.

Civic Activitation and Participation

Vogel and Triandafyllidou (2005) argue that a better understanding of the civic participation potential of immigrants would be important for Europe (and by extrapolation, for other receiving societies) at this time. International migration levels are expected to rise, even as there has been an overall decline in civic participation in general. The term 'civic activities' includes political participation as well as civil activities which span a wider range of community engagement. Vogel and Triandafyllidou (2005, p.3) define civic participation as consistently 'investing time and energy to organize solidarity or give a voice to societal concerns in the receiving society'. Civic activation participants or immigrant activists give voice to societal concerns by engagement in both public and informal collectivities. These include political parties, local committees, parent associations or immigrant lobbying organizations. Immigrant activists take up leadership functions in religious bodies, ethnic associations or community self-help networks in their activities to promote solidarity and self-help.

These authors have mentioned above (p.47) that only a minority of immigrants will be able or willing to take up demanding forms of civic activism. Yet, as change agents, their activities can have positive influence on the integration process and conditions of the wider communities. Activists are key persons in immigrant communities. The authors lay stress on the important value inputs which activists can make into the integration field. Vogel and Triandafyllidou (p.17) observe that more immigrant activism might be expected in societies where civic activities are generally promoted and wide-spread, while those with a weak culture of activism might not support immigrants to become active.

Culture

Clegg (2008, p.658) offers a description of culture as 'the totality of everyday knowledge that people use habitually to make sense of the world around them through patterns of shared meanings and understandings passed down through language, symbols, and artifacts'. Culture permeates the way we tend to think about and form understandings of migration, integration processes and immigrant groups. As a concept, it has also penetrated policy formation processes and integration programme implementation in different ways.

Phillip's (2007) observations are very pertinent to immigrant integration discourses that revolve around culture. The author draws attention to the problematic nature of the concept of cultures, which tend to be mistakenly understood as singular, unified and bounded entities. Pierik (2004) has referred to this as culturalistic fallacy. Phillips (2007, p.15) further questions the explanatory power so often attributed to cultures, pointing out that 'cultures are produced by people, rather than being things that explain why they behave the way they do'. Culture in its concrete and bounded conceptualization is a frame that can be used to reinforce oppressive practices and traditions. Moreover the over-use of 'culture' as a marker of minorities contributes to stereotyping. As first and foremost bearers of culture, members of minority groups can be projected as incapable of agency and determined by their culture. Žižek (2008) also refers to processes of culturalization, and in particular to the culturalization of politics which neutralizes political inequality or economic exploitation into cultural differences which cannot be overcome but only tolerated.

Ghorashi, Eriksen and Alghasi (2009) note that European discourse about new migrants is now a 'culturalist' one in which migrants' culture is thought to be a deviation from a European norm. Based on a static and essentialist understanding of culture, this approach holds culture and cultural content to be the determining factor underlying all actions of individuals. This way of thinking is blind to intra-group variations in groups with common national origins. The authors distinguish between the constructive use of categories and the abuse of categories when cultural categories are reified and create divisive and absolute contrasts between peoples. They state further that the dominance of culturalist framing of issues in Europe has led to a magnified focus on threatening elements of cultural difference and a widening rift in European societies between 'the European self and the migrant other' (2009, p.9). After 11 September 2001 events, religion has come to be dominant in the perceptions of the culture of others.

Ghorasi, Eriksen and Alghasi (2002) refer to Taylor's (1992) work on the importance of social recognition for individuals. Formal recognition would signify a secure space in society. As compared with having constantly to be on the defensive, new immigrant groups could afford to reflect, revisit their own cultural habitus impartially and even consider ways of how best to come to terms with new cultural elements. Ghorasi, Eriksen and Alghasi (2002) argue however, that allowing space for tolerance does not go far enough since we should also make and guard a common shared space for cultures where they can meet and connect with each other. This concern has affinity with Mernissi's (2000) call, which was mentioned in Chapter 2, for a secure space dedicated to providing opportunities for engaging with, confronting and removing traditions (tribal or cultural) which are associated with violence or discrimination. The defending of such a space would constitute defending the liberty and space of others, in accordance with democratic principles in the treatment of all citizens Ghorasi, Eriksen and Alghasi (2002).

In his book *The Arab Awakening*, Ramadan (2012, p.136) comments on the fear and mistrust being generated in the West by 'the presence of Muslims' who are being 'seen as a source of problems and of conflict'. Ramadan (2012, p.135) explains that Muslim population groups in settlement societies of the West, are basing their efforts of 'resistance to economic and cultural imperialism' in a 'religious substrate'. Thus religion, rather than culture, is being used as a springboard and social tool for negotiating the terms of incorporation and citizenship in ethnoculturally diverse settlement societies.

Immigrant settlement and integration can often be assumed to be processes in which new groups become inserted into an already existing, unified social order, featuring a homogeneous culture and set of values. Rudiger and Spencer (2003, p.4) remind us that the monolithic culture or social order is not a reality. In democratic societies, many different lifestyles, values and institutional arrangements are to be found. As Wieviorka (1998) also commented, these are moreover in a constant change process. Rudiger and Spencer (2003) state that assimilative thrusts towards conformity are badly off mark since conformity or uniformity does not exist in the wider society. Understanding integration processes as proceeding along a set trajectory is a mistake even though in many societies of immigration, implicit social and political pressures to assimilate persist. Rudiger and Spencer (2003) further point to the phenomenon which is fast gaining more recognition, namely, that pervasive pressure to conform can and does have the opposite effect, leading to reinforced social divisiveness and an accentuation of difference by minority groupings.

Cultural imperialism exists in an environment where the majority culture, or the culture of the ruling class has been established as the norm. It involves the universalization and establishment of a dominant group's experience and culture as the societal norm (Young, 1990). Specific group/s exercise of covert or overt power in society can through privileged access dominate the means of interpretation and communication in practice (see Fraser, 1987). Consequently the experience, values, goals and achievements of these groups are the most widely disseminated and come to prevail across society. Often without being conscious of it, dominant or majority groups project their own experience and ideas as the universal standard (Young, 1990).

Cultures can comprise a medium which allows people to link into other life styles and philosophies. Individuals who venture into cultures other than their own can thereby expand the territory of experience and learning. In the age of global migration and interpenetration, cultures are larger than issues of boundaries. The multicultural idea could be developed toward a recognition of the cumulative added value of diversities in societies of today.

Gateways

Scrutiny of new and old 'immigrant gateways' sheds light on differences in environments of resettlement and on settlement modes in these. The momentum of migration flows, including labour migration flows, means that old gateways will continue to attract migrants. However settlement will also take place in newer locations outside of the traditional urban concentrations. Waters and Jimenez (2005) direct attention to the fact that there are far fewer studies on newer gateways of arrival and settlement. Research is needed to explore how immigrants influence the social and economic landscape of communities which have not been accustomed to an immigrant presence.

The integration experience of immigrants coming to new gateways could be very different from that of those settling in more established gateways. In established gateways where immigrant communities have been settled for some time, their different positions in the class structure and in the ethnocultural hierarchies and map are already etched into the social fabric, as it were. On the other hand, in new gateways with little or less experience of immigration, the place of newcomers is undefined. This might constitute for the latter an opportunity to have more autonomy in defining their place in the surrounding society (Waters and Jimenez, 2005). However, the experience of immigrants in a new gateway is not necessarily one offering greater freedom in defining their position. Much depends on conditions in the receiving environment.

The settlement experience of immigrants settling into small communities is qualitatively different from urban settlement. A new gateway would not be able to offer established national or ethnocultural communities as a ready site of social interaction for newcomers. The scope for social interaction with compatriots is naturally smaller and limited by the overall community size, which could, but not necessarily, lead to a higher level of interaction between residents and newcomers. In the routine of everyday life, newcomers and older residents share common facilities which increase the likelihood of interaction and possibly reduce the risk of social isolation.

The resettlement of small groups of Vietnamese quota refugees in northerly Finnish towns in the late 1980s and early 1990s is an example of integration in new gateways. The newcomers were generally very well received and made lasting social ties with local people. However, the groups in these smaller communities and towns gradually dwindled as a result of secondary migration to larger population concentrations. Immigrants were drawn by several factors among which employment opportunity considerations were high. Apart from the greater likelihood of employment, 'pull' factors included the availability of seasonal employment in the farming sector, established religious congregations and already existing links into the larger ethnocultural community. This secondary movement showed characteristics of chain migration in that it was frequently facilitated by previous contacts and networks. Larger ethnocultural communities can lend background support to individuals undertaking settlement and integration tasks.

The established communities in the larger cities of Helsinki and Turku, for example, are characterized by diversity in different areas such as political allegiance, ethnicity, socioeconomic and educational background and religious affiliation. Individuals would have wider possibilities for rebuilding close social circles. Secondary migration might also be more common during downturns in the national economy when labour mobility becomes a jobseeking strategy for individuals. The findings of Rönnqvist's (2009, p.157) study of Vietnamese in Sweden indicate that secondary moves and ethnic networks serve as 'a path towards integration rather than an impediment to integration'. Subsequent secondary migration (in the same country) and transmigration (over a national border) offer migrants a way of widening the field of opportunity, or as is often the case, an alternative to limited scope in the initial site of settlement. Secondary migration should be viewed positively in the light of immigrants' ongoing pursuit of a satisfactory level of integration, and not least, an opportunity to be productive.

In general an attraction in established immigrant gateways is the range of reception and integration-oriented services. In addition to the basic service offers pertaining to health, education, social welfare and employment, old gateways can have well developed specialized facilities in interpreting, legal aid, information and referral, as well as immigrant community organizations which serve multifaceted integration functions as described above. Ethnocultural groups can grow through replenishment from different channels of immigration such as chain migration, marriage migration, family reunification or sponsorship of relatives (when this is allowed). Waters (1990) and Alba (1990) predict that if 'new' immigration to the groups diminishes, each successive generation born in the settlement country will have fewer contacts with immigrant generations. Ethnicity is likely to recede in order of importance in their lives.

Pro-Integration and Potentially Pro-integration Societal Characteristics

Historical events and processes help to shape integration-facilitating aspects in receiving societies. In old 'gateways', cities and locations have a tradition in immigrant arrivals and reception. Familiarity and accommodation with diversity have matured. There are usually old and new immigrant communities into which new arrivals can link. The argument of Kasinitz, Mollenkopf and Waters (2004) is that the Civil Rights Movement and New York City's history as an immigrant-absorbing community have left a legacy that has contributed positively to the ability of contemporary immigrants to feel included almost immediately and to regard themselves as New Yorkers.

Anthropologist Edward Hall's (1976) model[1] of high and low context cultures can shed some light on context-situated features of social relations. The author differentiates between types and densities of social relationship patterns which occur in social contexts. The 'pure types' at the poles of a high to low context culture continuum are presented here.

Along the social association continuum in high context cultures, social relationships develop gradually. These are stable and founded on trust, with a strong distinction between persons who are inside and outside one's personal circle. Personal relationships have great weight in guiding how decisions are made. An individual's identity is grounded in proximate groups such as family, work and culture. The social and authority structure is centralized with responsibility at the top and accepted as being at the top. The person or persons high on the hierarchy are perceived as having responsibility for the good of the others.

Social association mores in low context groups are located at the other end of the continuum. Relationships are more spontaneous and can have a shorter and more rapid span. An individual's circle is not carefully bounded and its composition more flexible and fluid. In general goals and procedures precede personal relations in dealing with matters and issues. Identity is person-based with emphasis on accomplishments. In low context environments, the social structure and responsibility is more decentralized. Responsibility does not rest at the top.

The model of high and low contexts presents pure or ideal types located at the extreme poles on a continuum of social association. Although in actuality these extremes are rare, the high-low context frame can shed some light on the processes of social encounter of settling immigrants. Low and high context patterns occur within the same environment and in different configurations. High and low context patterns can be observed in informal or private relations as well as in institutional settings. High context association can also be superimposed on organizational practice and norms.

For immigrants who are not positioned in networks, low context environments and institutions with more permeable boundaries can offer a more positive field of opportunity in settlement. This is probably another factor which pulls migrants towards larger cities where pockets of low context association are more likely to be found. On the other hand, we could hypothesize that high context environments which can learn to accept and accommodate persons

---

1 See Herberg, D.C., 1993. *Frameworks for Cultural and Racial Cultural Diversity.* Toronto: Canadian Scholars Press.

from the outside with some adjustment to their associational norms, would be advantageous associational fields for immigrants and newcomers.

Integration Shadows

One area of vulnerability experienced by settling immigrants and refugees is in their position of being non-subjects, the objects or targets of various processes in receiving societies. This generally passes unnoticed or is taken for granted among the majority, native, more dominant population groups. Even though newcomers might be socially resilient, they must be keenly aware of how social relations might be conducted in new environments. Their personal and socioeconomic progress through integration is often heavily affected or deflected by dispositions and social relations in the receiving society.

In the case of 'visible' groups, individuals must develop as best they can, appropriate defence mechanisms against the possibilities of racist capricious behaviours and everyday oppressive practices. Their mechanisms include cognitive or behavioural responses which can be either adequate or ineffective in ensuring that the individual maintains her/his personal and cultural integrity and dignity over time. Social support is a prime protective mechanism, particularly when it is proffered from majority or dominant group members, either consciously or spontaneously. Indeed solidarity extended from native, majority or dominant groups and their members is a precious anti-racism commodity in settlement and integration circumstances. It moreover contributes significantly to the quality of life aspects in settlement.

Stereotyping, summary categorizations, other misinformed actions combined with varying shades of self-interest are among the sometimes 'trivial' practices which add up cumulatively to systemic discrimination or peripheralization. This feature affects the integration processes of immigrants also in societies which confusingly protect vested social interests while professing constitutional and institutional principles of universal equality and social justice.

Handling Resistance in the Social Environment

Oppression is a familiar topic in social work and in studies of immigrant integration. Silvermint's (2013) study on resistance to oppression is presented here. It offers insight into how individuals might relate to oppressive treatment or how they might deal with their encounters with oppression. The discussion is relevant in the context of migrants' social integration challenges. Based a political philosophy perspective, Silvermint's (2013) article presents a thoughtful examination of why individuals might be personally responsible for resisting their own oppression and on what grounds, as victims, they might not be expected to resist. Selected points of salience from this work are presented and discussed here.

Silvermint (2013) observes that victims react to 'oppression' in different understandable ways. While some fight back, others prefer to believe that the obligation to deal with oppression falls entirely elsewhere. There are those who calculate that their best interests do not lie in resistance because of related risks or because compliance or complicity yield greater immediate benefits. Still others assess that the chances of resistance being effective are weak when the circumstances of oppression seem overwhelming.

Silvermint (2013, p.405) offers his view that 'oppression is a social circumstance that systematically and wrongfully burdens a victim's autonomy or overall life prospects'. Oppression is then an effect brought about cumulatively by various norms, actions, practices, and institutions. The nature of the effect is that it permeates nearly all domains of an individual's life stably over time. Resistance to someone or something can be understood as either opposing or counteracting (external resistance) or withstanding (internal resistance). Discussions relating to the obligation to resist generally refer to external resistance.

Silvermint (2013) further illustrates how ways of grounding the obligation to resist will influence the kind of resistance response that will be evoked. If for example the obligation to resist is based on the idea that non-resistance signals acceptance of oppressive norms or institutions, resistance will call for a public gesture of taking a stand in a manner that clearly communicates what the individual is standing for. Should the obligation to resist be based on the idea that resistance is solely a matter of a self-respecting, autonomous response to oppression, the stand then taken could be viewed as a personal instead of the public matter.

Silvermint (2013, p.406) proposes that 'engaging in resistance is good for victims as well as necessary for leading a morally worthwhile life'. Despite the fact that considerations of wellbeing sometimes justify non-resistance, the neglect of one's own wellbeing through compliance or complicity is difficult to justify. The author contends that in almost any conception of wellbeing, one cannot lead a morally worthwhile, flourishing life without self-respect and autonomy.

Self-respect means an understanding of one's inherent dignity and non-acceptance of affronts to that dignity. Individuals see themselves as equals in the moral community of persons, as persons entitled to a certain threshold of treatment by others. Another aspect of self-respect is the individual's own appreciation of the significance of being a moral agent, of acting in ways that correspond to her/his standards of self-respect and taking her/his responsibility seriously.

Autonomy means self-direction. Even though they are not free of social influence, autonomous agents have the inclination and the capacity to live their lives as they see fit, to select and act on aims of their own choosing instead of having their decisions externally determined in ways that obstruct life plans or hinder self-definition' (Silvermint, 2013, p.418).

It is evident that self-respect and autonomy are beneficial for individuals, and in particular, for those who face oppression. Self-respect and autonomy are necessary for the successful pursuit and meaningful enjoyment of most valuable aims, and for feeling authentic satisfaction with how one's life is going. Moreover, 'In oppressive circumstances, resistance is intrinsically good for victims because engaging in resistance *just is* a self-respecting, autonomous response to oppression' (Silvermint, 2013, p.407). The author emphasizes that resisting is important both for the sake of asserting one's status to others, and for affirming it to oneself. To rely solely on internal resistance is likely to underestimate the damaging effect that oppression can do to an individual's self-conception.

As Individuals and Newer Citizens

Societies are organized differently with respect to how they cater to the needs of their citizens. In some societies the state takes a very minimal role in responding to needs in its population. The family, their informal networks and organized bodies in civil society have a central role in catering to need. In other societies the state is a central actor not only in providing for needs but also in honouring social security guarantees against risks such as sickness, unemployment and old age. When immigrants enter these systems, they seek acceptance on the same terms designated in the particular societies in which they settle.

In the context of social change, service responses and policy interpretations do not keep up immediately with changing needs and it is to be expected that a degree of mismatch or lagging can occur in different areas of service provision. In immigrant receiving societies, rights cater in principle to all population groups, but the forms and measures through which they are implemented might be only partially relevant or appropriate to the effective fostering of integration. Generally material settlement needs have been easier to meet. Those 'needs' relating to insertion in the socioeconomic area of the labour market and other competitive areas in education seem still to be contentious issues in receiving societies even in those with longer histories of immigration.

Formal rights have not been effective in preventing social marginalization of immigrant groups. In the literature on integration there is abundant evidence that in many systems with declared social citizenship rights, immigrants do not fare as well as majority groups. This holds true even after immigrants might have resided for lengthy periods in the countries of settlement. The uneven outcomes of rights are evident in immigrant groups especially in the area of the labour market, where they can be peripheralized for indefinite periods. When rights are not effectively and directly enforced or enforceable, as, for example, when mechanisms to guarantee them do not exist or do not function, the individual is a bearer of rights which cannot be operationalized. To explain this predicament in the context of rights, we can say that their civil rights to socially just treatment are out of reach.

Societal Legitimacy

In this chapter I am making an argument that the majority of obstacles to effective integration is linked to the fact that 'societal legitimacy' for immigrants is weak and would need to be addressed. In the midst of a sea of 'rights' many immigrants and immigrant groupings find themselves situated disproportionately along the periphery of the socioeconomic mainstream. This theme is not new in migration studies and many explanations have been generated by researchers of migrant receiving countries over the latter twentieth century up to the present time. Frames such as social exclusion, racism, oppression, culturalization and monopoly treat with the social and institutional dynamics of these processes that seem to self-protect from modern demographic changes using very personal and local mechanisms. Segmented assimilated theory seeks to capture the underlying dynamics of new minority marginalization even into the succeeding generation in economically developed welfare societies.

In his research on the relationship between belonging and entitlement (Skey, 2014, p.327) distinguishes between groups who enjoy 'ontological security' and those who might not. Skey (2014) presents Giddens (1990) definition of ontological security as referring to 'the confidence that most human beings have in the continuity of their self-identity and in the constancy of the surrounding social and material environments of action' (Giddens, 1990, p.92). Skey (2014) describes the ontologically secure as those who assume to be and are treated as if they 'really' belong in the nation. This status of 'really belonging' endows persons with certain privileges relative to others. Skey (2014, p.327) argues that while providing individuals with 'an important sense of agency, in an era where growing numbers feel increasingly disenfranchised', 'really belonging' also prompts powerful claims to social, economic and cultural resources. In other words, there is a strong link between belonging and entitlement'. Belonging becomes conflated with deserving.

The sense of entitlement yields tangible as well as intangible psycho-social prerogatives of power to feel secure and understood, to understand and thus to be able to be a judge of the behaviour of 'others', and so on. Skey (2014, p.328) reflects on the 'valued and grounded sense of self, place and community' that belonging to the nation generates, which can explain why 'challenges to it are so passionately debated and, often, resisted' in the face of change or perceived threats of change in the society.

I argue here that peripheral status of new citizens and population groups can be seen to be one in which citizenship *legitimacy* is weak. Individuals or groups are simply not acknowledged as being justified to exercise equal participation rights. Their rights can be evaded since their claims are not taken as being justified. They might enjoy social security and rights to social welfare and services, but on the labour market, visible minorities might remain largely invisible in mainstream paths and occupations. The calls for recognition and inclusion really are about being accepted into the polity and societal field and treated fairly as people who are indeed *socially justified* to claim participation rights on a par with others. This probably would not remove self-interest based discrimination which takes place in most groups across the fields of competitive social life. However if those with immigrant background and different ethnocultural origins are seriously treated as socially justified to participate *on a par* with others, 'different' groups would be less disproportionally relegated by non-formal mechanisms to the societal periphery. This discussion is about a covert dimension of social citizenship that differentiates between the institutional relations enjoyed by established groups and those whose formal membership is not substantively and fully acknowledged.

Societies can measure themselves on their range of 'rights' which recognize citizens' needs, membership in the polity, and entitlements to make claims and redeem their rights. Comparative international studies generally reflect formal legislation, policy and rights which are in place to frame immigrant settlement and integration. Social citizenship rights are in principle a culturally neutral instrument for extending certain entitlements and guarantees in society's political, civil and social spheres in an equal manner across the citizenry. The covert dimension of citizenship rights described above is elusive and has not yet been measured or acknowledged. However it pervades all areas of exclusion and should be urgently addressed if societies are to cohere, and if their newer citizens brought into the national community.

Chapter 4
Policy and Institutions

Introduction

This chapter examines different aspects of policymaking. Social work is involved in different ways of policymaking processes right through to the implementation and evaluation stages. Immigration and integration policies are sensitive to demographic changes. Societies new to immigration must integrate new policy instruments alongside other more established policy frames. The input and feedback of social work into immigration and integration policy processes is important because practitioners constantly use, apply and adapt policy instruments to the presenting settlement situations in the field. They are aware of how policy affects service user situations not only immediately but over time. They have an ideal perspective on how policy actually functions. The profession has a central place in policy processes.

There has been a tendency for research to focus on ideal types of immigrant integration which obscure the complexity of phenomena. Inevitably this imposes limits on the approaches to policy, as well as the understandings, interpretations and implementation of it. Scholten's (2011) work examined public policies on immigrant integration. He argues that the development of better policies will call for moving beyond disciplinary boundaries and assumptions so that multiple contesting frames might be brought to bear on policy making processes in this area. Policy can be strengthened by a wider range of input from different disciplinary perspectives. Scholten's (2011) view is understandable because of the nature of the migrant integration phenomenon. Integration represents a holistic engagement with the whole of society and policy responses would be enhanced by relevant knowledge and understandings across disciplines and institutional sectors.

One important aspect which can be lost in formal policymaking is that of migrants' personal aspirations and goals which are the critical factors for giving impetus and motivation to integration efforts. Incorporation has been conceptualized, from Freeman's (2004, p.945) 'radically dis-aggregated perspective', as a process taking place at the intersection of migrant aspirations and strategies with the society's regulatory frameworks in the four domains of the state, market, welfare and culture. We can question here whether it is possible for integration policy and programme initiatives to be effective if migrants' own aspirations are incidental to the process.

Favell (1998, p.3) sees the term 'integration' as portraying 'progressive-minded, tolerant and inclusive approaches to dealing with ethnic minorities'. This author makes the observation that the fundamental question concerns more than just 'the integration of new ethnic minorities'. Integration is also a question about the 'glue' of a society holding together its wider cultural, regional and class divisions. Immigration raises 'as a live political issue', the 'more general question about the unity and order of the nation, and the public myths and traditions that hold it together' (Favell, 1998, p.3). Immigration debates are politically charged since they simultaneously spark off fundamental question of national cohesion among majority groups who are faced with the need to update their understandings of the nation and polity, and to come to terms with their own position in relation to these.

Integration policy has often been seen as a range of measures and particular rules for helping immigrants to develop the skills needed to manage in a new society. It takes places in a context of a two way process involving adaptation of newcomers to the social and structural environment as well as institutional adaptation to facilitate the incorporation of new groups. Integration can also be viewed as a two-way interchange of culture and understanding in which the receiving community and institutions as well as the immigrants must adapt (Phillimore and Goodson, 2008). Adaptation processes of immigrants have been examined extensively in qualitative and quantitative research across many disciplines.

Institutional and structural change in receiving societies has been studied from the perspective of formal measures put in place nationally and cross-nationally to facilitate integration. These changes take place in different ways and to different degrees within national and local administrative and service provision contexts. Institutional and structural changes for accommodating new groups in the population would need to be evaluated regularly for effectiveness in a constantly evolving integration situation. Quantitative surveys yield one important level of data, but findings from studies on the ground in the communities would contribute authentic input which would be critical for keeping programmes on track.

The institutions of the receiving society have great bearing on the quality and outcome of settlement. Institutions mediate settlement through provision of services, information, rights and entitlements. Moreover they are also the formally positioned and empowered initiators for overall change and adjustment in practices which will aim to improve service responses to meet the needs of newcomer citizens. The critical administrative role and reach of institutions influences both directly and indirectly how societal relations will tend to be structured between majority and minority groups, and how constructive these relations will be.

Penninx (2003) states that the functioning of general public institutions and the manner in which they adjust to diversity in the population, are of high importance in the promotion or obstruction of access and for equitable integration outcomes. Institutions include the educational system, for example, and the institutional arrangements in the labour market. Laws, regulations, and executive organizations together with their unwritten rules and practices form part of such institutions

The power asymmetry between the critical mass of institutions and minority groups is one factor relating to the great effort needed to realize change, including positive change, in established practices. On the other hand the stability of institutions work to safeguard a level of functional consistency, securing and ensuring a rhythm and patterns in their specialized activity areas in the society. Civil society can be seen as comprising its own institutional structure but these are non-state and non-market entities which enjoy varying degrees of status and influence in the society. Immigrant community organizations can succeed in representing their constituencies' interest if they are well placed and organized.

Integration processes take place at the local level in a wide range of local contexts. Local policies need to be built on active interaction between immigrants and local society in order to ensure that they are appropriate to the prevailing local conditions of integration (Penninx, 2003). In practice this means that integration-oriented policies, strategies and actions should be based on engagement with immigrants whose wellbeing and integration the policies target. This approach is radically different from that in which interaction is viewed as a transaction between client/service receiver and administrator.

Patterns of social integration can be markedly different without any of these being either better or worse than the others (Rudiger and Spencer, 2003). The nature of policy is such that it allows for a certain degree of flexibility in interpretation and application. This is a distinct advantage because the contextual conditions in which policies are to be applied, are varied. Policies are generally meant to be adaptable in different scenarios. Policies are concretized, operationalized and, to a point, 'standardized' through set frameworks of regulations and rules. Skillful and enlightened policy interpretation and application will be faithful to the thrust of the policy while maximizing the benefits to be gained from policy initiatives. At the level of implementation, the policy process call for resources of skill, experience and insight in policy interpretation and utilization on the ground.

Many political, resource and municipal level factors might bring about a policy dilution process. The potential, spirit and original intent of the policy might not survive through the implementation stage. The gap between policy and practice, between rhetoric and reality often arises from what subsequently does not or does take place. Evaluation activity and strategic feedback is crucial for carrying through policy effectively and for the ongoing viability of the policy implementation process.

Welfare, Wellbeing and Thriving as Goals of Integration

Social welfare is fundamental to integration processes. It is organized societies' structure-based instrument which responds to basic needs of individuals. The 'Basic Rights Argument' elaborated by Shue (1996) is directly salient to social welfare systems. The author's central thesis is that everyone has 'basic rights' to 'security' and 'subsistence'. These basic rights are essential if other rights are to be enjoyed. For all other (non-basic) rights to be enjoyed, basic rights need to be in place. Basic rights are neither more valuable nor more satisfying that other rights. Beitz and Goodin (2009) point to the possibility that a non-basic right such as freedom of speech, for example, might contribute more to a person's capacity for achieving what she or he might value as important in life. Thus the exercise of this non-basic right might produce more satisfaction than a 'basic right'.

Organized welfare is held to reach its peak in welfare states because of the scope and 'generosity' levels of social insurance, benefits and services. State welfare provision is organized and resourced to provide a level of security and subsistence far above that of the minimal 'safety net'. However in the field of immigrant integration in particular, it would be important to set social welfare in broader contexts of wellbeing. The concept of wellbeing, like that of basic rights, recognizes the primal importance of individuals' ability to meet basic needs. Maslow's (1943) familiar hierarchy of needs differentiates between so-called 'lower order' and 'higher order needs'. My argument is that the focus in social welfare systems can grow to be too narrowly focused and specialized in responding to lower order needs for food, housing, and safety. It is undeniable that organized welfare responses to these needs and their related rights are most valuable in freeing individuals to attend to and work autonomously toward higher order needs such as self-realization. It is a general assumption that once settling immigrants have material security, they will be well equipped to engage in their autonomous pursuits to become fully participating members of the society. The gap between entitlement to basic welfare security and access to resources and opportunities to make progress towards meaningful participation roles and self-realization goals can be quite stark. Glass ceilings and fences are metaphors that reflect this inability to pursue self-development goals in a societal sense.

When we look at the role of material welfare in overall immigrant integration, its pivotal role is undeniable. Yet without the realization of their participatory goals in valued and value-contributing areas of mainstream society, the value of an achieved level of material welfare becomes fragile in the long term, because it cannot generate for settling persons a satisfactory level of meaningfulness as social beings. It is argued here that the appreciation and enjoyment of material welfare provision will grow in an exponential fashion with individuals' ability to realize their self-development as well as productivity and participatory goals in settlement society. This needs to be recognized in welfare states which after considerable investment in welfare provision, stop short of instituting other 'tougher' measures to bring about fair terms of societal participation for newer citizens.

It would be advantageous to retain focus on human and civil rights dimensions alongside social rights in the discourse and, not least, in the policy agenda. Alongside social welfare rights, civil and economic rights would be of central importance for immigrant integration. In economically developed receiving countries with sophisticated welfare systems, immigrants' problems with access to economic opportunity in the labour market are not framed as a weakness in civil rights to justice. Labour market marginalization is discussed in terms of 'oppression', 'discrimination' or 'racism'. They are seen as anomalies (albeit widespread) in the system, which possibly require extraordinary shifts if they are to be addressed effectively. In actuality, these could equally be portrayed and understood as basic problems with civil rights to social justice. In economic phrasing, individuals lack 'life chances' or access to opportunities, a condition which eventually leads to enforced dependency on welfare. Interventions to address civil rights infringements are likely to stand a better chance of being justifiable and prioritizable on the national policy agenda. The politics of interventions would be situated in an area less susceptible to contention.

Membership and Citizenship

Membership and citizenship are sometimes used interchangeably in integration discourse. Both refer to national belonging but it is possible to differentiate between them. Citizenship is more of an official or formal status or category to which certain rights are attached. Membership on the other hand can be seen in contemporary usage as implying ties of some type with other members. Guild, Groenendijk and Carrera (2009, p.2) are uniting these two in referring to EU 'member states attempting to keep intact their discretionary powers over the understanding and normative framing of their 'community of citizens'.

The question of what type of citizenship is being envisaged for immigrants is a pertinent one for policy. The citizenship problematic can be further broken down into formal and substantive citizenship. Persons without formal citizenship or permission to reside can be extended some level of basic services, such as, for example, in the case of asylum seekers awaiting refugee determination decisions. Immigrants who are in settlement processes will be affected by their access to participatory spheres such as education and employment as well as their social rights benefits, social security and insurance, and social services. Policymaking entails overall charting of social welfare provisioning, health, housing, schooling, education and labour market training needs. Immigrant integration engages the input, interaction and collaboration of many sectors of public policy.

On another tier of integration a pertinent issue relates to *what positions are envisaged for immigrants in the opportunity structure*. This participatory area is key to quality of life and the meeting of needs for self-development and self-fulfilment as well as economic independence and the autonomy it brings. It is also an area that reflects whether citizenship is formal or substantive. Individuals wish to achieve their potential, to have a view of this for the future, to achieve robust and respected roles in society, alongside all other citizens.

The gap between the range of functionings of an individual and her capacity set is one way of appraising quality of life. The 'capabilities approach' is a theoretical position in political philosophy and development economics. It was originally proposed by Amartya Sen (1999) and Martha Nussbaum (1999). It presumes that all individuals have a set of potential 'functionings', the various things which a person might value doing or being. These 'beings' and 'doings' range from being nourished and healthy, to participating in community life and enjoying respect. Capabilities are the substantive freedoms to achieve alternative valued functioning configurations which are constitutive of valuable lives. An individual's capabilities are the positive freedoms and opportunities he or she can access. These are reflections of egalitarian justice.

If the gap between functionings and capabilities is unbridgeable in a chronic way by immigrants, this is a sign that their human capital is discounted. This phenomenon can be common not only in periods when there is a situation of job scarcity or economic downturn in the wider society. Immigrants tend to be disproportionately represented among jobless groups, which is in turn a function of labour market practices disadvantageous to newcomers and immigrants. When migrant youth face the long term prospect of this type of status in society, their perception is decidedly negative since it is based on the frame of life experience occurring in their own homeland. Contemporary societies and their integration regimes must contend with youth alienation that should be seen as not only occurring, but as brought about, in their midst.

Sen's (1999) capability approach focuses on doings and beings and on the freedom to achieve them instead of the goods or resources which people can possess. Young (1990) has pointed out that justice cannot be reduced to the distribution of goods. In Young's (1990) concept of justice, the equitable distribution of the basic necessities, goods, luxuries and burdens is not enough as people should be able to participate also in the decision-making processes that shape particular patterns of distribution in the first place. Fair and equitable distribution of goods and bads is a basic element of justice. However when some groups are shut out of distributional activity and processes and situated solely at the receiving end through systemic processes, this constitutes injustice despite the fact that distributional processes aim to be equitable. One of Young's (1990, p.19) main contentions has been that contemporary theorists of justice narrow their focus to issues of wealth and income distribution but give scant attention to urgent issues such as 'the right to meaningful work, control over one's community, the division of labor, and issues of power within the family'.

The Societal Profile of Citizenship

Integration is understood as leading to representation of immigrants or newer citizens across the society. This refers to their active participation in the economic, political, civic, social and cultural life of the society. Roles need to be open to newcomers in the public spheres in education, labour market, and other areas of institutional life. The non-portability of previously earned qualifications and experience is a significant stumbling block, noticeable particularly among more highly educated immigrants. In equitable conditions, immigrants would be represented proportionately in roles of all types and at all levels, horizontally and vertically in the society. They would be visible in the public life spheres as agents, contributors, decision-makers and societal stakeholders. This would call for policy that would actually open up existing career paths to immigrants and minorities by facilitating equitable and open competition along upward as well as lateral mobility trajectories.

Rudiger and Spencer (2003) state that the social and economic status of migrants and ethnic minorities is a foremost indicator of their overall integration into society, and of the degree of equality and cohesion in the particular society. Socioeconomic integration is portrayed and can be measured by migrants' equal and proportional participation and representation in the areas of employment, education, health and housing. According to Rudiger and Spencer (2003), indicators which measure socioeconomic positions according to their *vertical* distribution, i.e. income, qualification, job seniority, access to health care, quality of housing etc., place a stronger emphasis on equality. For immigrant integration, these are critically important indicators. Other indicators of horizontal distribution, e.g. labour market segmentation, proportion of migrants in particular schools or residential areas, shed light on the factor of diversity. The usefulness of indicators for social and economic policymaking is increased if they can shed light on the circumstances of different groups of migrants by differentiating data according to gender, race/ethnicity, nationality and religion (Rudiger and Spencer, 2003).

Aspirations of Migrants

As mentioned above, Freeman (2004) perceives immigrants' aspirations and strategies as being of central significance in incorporation processes. Policymaking processes generally hold some form of stakeholder consultation exercises as a preliminary to the whole activity. These exercises might be considered as valuable opportunities for obtaining input or as formal procedures that in practice are somewhat peripheral to the policy process. Much depends on the capacity in which migrant advisory boards function in relation to main policymaking processes and also on the way these are constituted. With the exception of very new immigrant gateways, immigrants and their communities have acquired though residence, considerable experience and knowledge of the surrounding society, its people and its institutions. Migrants are also the individuals whose needs are being targeted and who are most aware of the nature of those needs.

What should integration policy promote and whose perspectives should be given weight in the policymaking process? Can the aspirations of immigrants converge with integration aims (of the majority) or are they generally irreconcilable with the whole undertaking? Although the State and government usually carry leading responsibility in policy formulation and implementation, the input of immigrants and other stakeholding organizations and institutions should be seriously taken into account in the policy-making process.

In a study of how multicultural policies operated in Australia, Canada and Sweden, Inglis (1996) observed that while ethnic minority groups were not the sole advocators of policy change, the ability of minority group members to influence policy decision-making was important. Members of ethnic minorities who participated in the policy-making process were found to be alert to the importance of overcoming economic and social disadvantage as a prerequisite for improving the status of ethnic minorities, even as they sought to maintain traditional cultures.

According to Inglis (1996) ethnic minority groups might have far more pragmatic attitudes about the importance of social equality than is assumed at times by those who criticize the culturalist emphases in the multicultural model. Pragmatic attitudes are illustrated in Eastmond's (2011) study of refugee integration in Sweden. Resettling refugees found that re-training and orientation programmes that form part of initial integration procedures unduly delayed their entry into the labour market. They would have preferred instead measures that supported them in using the personal skills and resources that they already possessed to established new lives in Sweden. Eastmond (2011, p.283) states that the 'introduction' regime, long criticized for its standardized formula with little room for individual variation and control, undermines the neoliberal goal of personal initiative and freedom of choice'.

Welfare States

As a major innovation in social welfare organization and delivery, the welfare state has been and continues to be the subject of much research and evaluation. More recently studies have been directed to its role in immigrant incorporation and to ways in which this particular welfare model might hinder or facilitate this process, given the particularities in arrangements in each national system.

The welfare state model evolved with the development of social democratic ideologies and social welfare capitalism. Wimmer 1998a points out that in addition to being a nation, a citizenry and a sovereignty, the people became a group of solidarity in their welfare state. With the establishment of national welfare states, the nationalist project attained its culmination. The author notes that membership in this group of solidarity was in the nature of a privilege, and the limitation of access to these privileges was marked by state boundaries.

Wimmer and Glick-Schiller (1992, p.310) consider some of the implications of immigration for national welfare state systems. Migrants in a sense, 'intrude' into a national space that has been carefully built on solidarity and indeed fuelled by it. In labour migration countries, the work process and relations for which migrants were recruited means that they should be included at some level into the system. The problem is how to include members who might carry different 'risks' and not fit into the standard categories of need. How would the welfare state cope in diversity?

Welfare states are characterized by complexity of organization which must be structured on elaborate systems of categories. Handelman (1976, p.234) states that decisions are predicated on categorical ascriptions of clients which define their entitlements and obligations. These bureaucratic categories reflect convenient images in which people, as objects of policy, are defined. They are set to portray a given type of case and are seldom arbitrary.

Research has uncovered in Nordic welfare states serious limitations in challenging racism and ethnic discrimination. The relegation of service users to clienthood roles has possibly had a constricting influence on immigrant service users, especially if they are in the position of enforced dependency due to joblessness and other situations that cause individuals to have to use the last resort of income support.

The integration paradox in the mature expanded welfare state is that its reach is comprehensive with the State providing the breadth of services which immigrants need in the initial stages of settlement. This in effect means that initially, social interface and contacts are to a great extent clustered on interface primarily with professional and official service providers. Interaction with the surrounding society takes place in schools, shops and other informal venues when these become familiar to newcomers. Although as Coffey (2004, p.2) notes, 'social policies can be made, enacted and implemented within and outside the auspices of the State', in expansive welfare states the State is the primary welfare provider with lesser roles for civil society and the market. There are welfare states which have designated space for civil society providers to participate in integration activity, which has greatly facilitated newcomer contacts with laypersons out in the communities from the outset of settlement.

The structure of the institutional welfare state is strengthened internally by its position power, its central placement in many spaces in the lives of citizens. It has derived its staying power from **solidary** support based on reciprocal arrangements with all citizens who are covered through their entitlements and their obligations. As taxpayers, citizens fulfil their obligations which are reciprocated in services, benefits and insurance. Nordic welfare states were ambitious in design and vision. They were very appropriate responses to conditions in the societies at the time in which they were developed and expanded to cover risks, contingencies and scarcity in the citizenry.

Immigrants are at a disadvantage as new or 'late' entrants to the labour market in welfare states. Welfare state benefits and social insurance are differentiated according to an individual's relationship to the labour force. Freeman (1986, p.51) states that 'within its boundaries the rhetoric of the welfare state is universal, but its practice is not'.

Freeman (1986) notes that the dual basis upon which benefits may be claimed, carries important consequences for migrant labour and newer citizens. In the context of gender inequality, the postindustrial welfare state can prevent poverty and exploitation but still tolerate severe gender inequality (Fraser, 1994; Tuori, 2007). Bolzonaro (2010) has emphasized the need for the link between precarious employment and the welfare state to be studied and explained. Freeman (1986, p.51) points out that the two tier system of benefits includes migrants into the social protection system but 'at the same time it fragments the beneficiary population into groups of citizens and noncitizens, workers and nonworkers'. The welfare state penalizes those who are outside the category of lifetime earnings. This also holds true at the pension stage when entitlements continue to be correspondingly minimal into old age.

Changing Policy and Programmes to Respond to Diversity in User Populations

The reshaping of policy to be sensitive to new conditions and new needs in the population invariably is a complex and time consuming process. A perennial issue is over the pros and cons of choosing radical, middle range or incremental change to existing legal and policy instruments. It is seldom that radical change is seen as feasible, sustainable or desirable. Policies and practices tend to lag behind different types of social change which take place continuously if not rapidly in society. This provides a partial explanation of why integration policies cannot be current with developments in migration patterns and settlement trends. The welfare state has been built to be a stable symbol of national solidarity and is moreover a highly complex functional entity. The challenge of changing policy is demanding even when it would be critical, logical and efficient to respond to changed conditions of need. It is almost predictable that policymakers will often resort to incremental changes. Not least, politicians also must think of their electorates and the limits of their term in office.

Charles Lindblom's (1959) essay, 'The Science of "Muddling Through"' heralded at the time a new approach to understanding public policy. Lindblom (1959) rejected the rational, comprehensive model of decision-making that required careful articulation of all goals and full consideration of all alternatives. This involved procuring, analysing and synthesizing large amounts of information, data and knowledge. The steps of a rational process of policy making included looking at and ranking all related values, as well as a comprehensive analysis of all possible policy outcomes, after which policymakers are in a position to make a choice that would be held to be in keeping with important values. Lindblom (1959) observed that this often is not possible in organizations and institutions. Considering the cognitive limitations of decision makers and conflicts occurring over values in policymaking, Lindblom argued that it was not rational to undertake rational, comprehensive decisions in policymaking (1959) and proposed that making small policy changes is often superior to making radical ones.

An incremental approach to policy decision-making telescopes the process. Policymakers consider a small number of alternatives for addressing a problem. Options are chosen which differ only marginally from existing policy. The level of 'risk'/uncertainty involved is low. Of significance is that *for each alternative, only the most important consequences are considered*. The concern with underlying values is not raised in the incremental model and there need not be consensus on values among policymakers. Thus in practice the policy's 'correctness' lies in coming to an agreement on the choice of option. The appropriate test of good policy becomes the ability to make a decision. A good policy is one that all participants agree on rather than what is best to solve a problem. Incrementalist policymaking involves configurations of value and policy trade-offs and compromises.

In Lindblom's (1959) model values are assumed to filter into the policymaking process through the different participating policymakers who represent the value based priorities of their own agencies and institutions. Thus we can see that participation and representation in such initial levels of decision-making processes is also essential if specific value positions are to be part of the processes. In this model, policy-making tends to be serial, since it requires revisiting problem areas as error or faults become apparent. New approaches to the issues are developed during the course of policy. The model suggests that larger changes occur gradually through a series of small steps, which is an alternative to 'rocking the boat'. In essence, the incremental model is remedial, focusing on small changes to existing policies rather than sweeping or fundamental changes.

Lindblom's (1959) claims regarding incrementalism's effectiveness have been neither established nor refuted. There is still controversy over whether changing the status quo by a series of small steps is beneficial. At the time it was introduced, critics raised concerns that 'incrementalism' might be a poor alternative to needed social innovation, or that it might reinforce 'inertia' in public organizations. The concept of adaptive management is based on an expanded version of the incremental approach. In adaptive management, the policies goals are made explicit and policies are treated as experiments. If progress is made toward the goal, the experiment is deemed successful. Adaptive management includes a measurement program which is the mechanism for assessing whether or not the policy/experiment is successful. The experimental stage corresponds to that of a pilot project stage which generates advance information on how a policy might perform in practice. This is an area which would be suitable to social work research. It would generate professional social work inputs into policymaking processes and help in the development of policy frames for the field.

The concept of 'bounded rationality' portrays a particular decision-making characteristic when people shortcut the steps in rational decision-making and in practice use the limited amount of the information which they have available at the time to make decisions (March and Simon, 1993). Bounded rationality can help to elucidate one aspect of the incrementalist process of decision-making. Both constitute more brief approaches towards decision-making in order to condense the procedures of the rational model.

Jansson (2003) observes that administrators and legislators might lean toward introducing modest changes in existing policies mainly in response to complaints or pressures. On the other hand, decision-makers both in agency and legislative settings are themselves often in support of making more significant changes to existing policy. Important revisions of programmes or the enactment of major social reform are sometimes proposed by legislators.

Exclusionary Mechanisms at Micro and Macro Level in the Labour Market

There are multiple reasons why participation in the labour market is for most people a crucial path not only to a satisfactory level of economic security, but to robust standing in the community. Employment is 'a mechanism for economic advancement and also serves many functions such as helping to establish social roles, develop language and cultural understanding, social connections and a sense of security' (Phillimore, 2008, p.314). Most importantly, the employment of adults has strong repercussions for family and in particular, youth wellbeing and welfare in the short and long term. For the individual, employment is a chance for onward and/or upward social mobility providing that labour market practices are equitable. The implementation of access-facilitating policy in the labour market in a key factor for integration and social inclusion.

Rudiger and Spencer (2003) state that there persists a lack of understanding of the indirect and institutional forms discrimination can assume. Generally anti-discrimination measures are thought of as comprising social or educational initiatives along with a ban on direct discrimination. Wider policies to address barriers to equality of opportunity in recruitment, promotion and retention are hardly evident in organizations and companies (Rudiger and Spencer, 2003). Direct discrimination is usually defined very narrowly in policy, although it can take many forms in organizations. Without specific targeting policies and effective instruments for identifying, investigating and addressing inequitable hiring and workplace practices, there is no constraining mechanism on covert forms.

Evans and Harris (2004, p.871) comment that 'the proliferation of rules and regulations should not automatically be equated with greater control over professional discretion; paradoxically, more rules may create more discretion'. This leaves an open field for discretion to work, or to be used, either way. Based on the findings of her study of the Somali community in the UK, Hammond (2013) concludes that the weak social position and poor performance of Somalis on educational and employment indicators of integration have more to do with discrimination and bureaucratic exclusion than with people opting out of integration processes.

Unemployment signifies a severe reversal of the active participatory processes that are vital to immigrant integration. There are *'grey areas'* which exist in the midst of formal equality legislation, policies and rules. In these ambiguous areas, guidelines and authority are not clear and controls are often weak. Often it is in principle not expedient to lay down very narrowly defined rules of procedure. In hiring and selection processes, for example, grey areas allow room for 'interpretation', 'discretion' and 'justification'. The power of interpretation and responsibility for deciding on the choice between 'correct', 'fair' or 'compromised' procedure lies squarely with the individuals or the leadership involved.

Sen (1997) has pointed out that chronic unemployment can affect an individuals' capacity for agency and increase the risk that their sphere of formal and informal influence will gradually shrink. Moreover, as Freeman (1986) has pointed out, it is an individual's employment history of earned income and income-based welfare contributions which determine in a decisive way, her/his level of social security, benefits, insurance and eventually pensions. Unemployment has a long reach into individuals' life quality.

Discrimination can be overt or covert, open or concealed. Scenarios of discrimination can adapt to context. There is a large body of literature available on this topic. However it would be useful to focus here on 'self-interest' driven discrimination which is somewhat different from that of 'privileged' circles. It is likely that individuals who 'do discrimination' are not necessarily racist or anti-immigration. It is often a *routine* question of gaining or retaining eased access to opportunity and by-passing in some way those competitive processes which would effectively widen the pool of applicants. These ways of doing discrimination routines speak more to self-interest motives. The style of operation requires a degree of complicity in the particular settings in which they occur in organizations, boards, committees, faculties, agencies and others. Due to the covert nature of doing discriminations, it generally operates in restricted circles. Alternatively they might be seen as networks of bounded and enforceable social capital for protecting turf (Coleman, 1988). When widely practiced, these 'pockets' cumulatively add up to a phenomenon of systemic exclusion or sometimes a form of segregation from the valued productive areas and tiers of opportunity in society. In public institutions and entities, where the 'goods' or jobs are not in private possession or private ownership, discriminatory practices can be seen in the light of misappropriation.

Immigrants and newcomers are at much greater disadvantage than locals when such forms of discrimination are inbuilt into structures in the society. This can be marked in newer immigrant gateways where immigration and diversity are novel phenomena of the recent decades. Compared with locals, immigrants' social networks are established over a much shorter time, and do not include the strong personal links into the labour market needed for penetrating different employment areas.

Although receiving societies usually have included some anti-discrimination provisions in their laws, *independent* public equality bodies have more seldom been established. Independent public equality bodies can act to enforce legal provision, whose mandate is defined in law. In their report on immigrant social integration and policies to combat discrimination, Rudiger and Spencer (2003) point out that one of the most enduring challenges to the effectiveness of anti-discrimination laws is the persistence of inequality in institutional policies and practices. The authors state that this should be addressed by legislation that moves beyond the principle of prohibiting discrimination to impose a positive duty to promote equality.

The Effects of Discrimination

Continuous interface with inequitable everyday practice in society sabotages migrants' integration efforts. Labour market thresholds raised by the non-portability of qualifications and experience are a denial of the achievements and merits of individuals who have invested considerable personal and material resources in skills acquisition and professional training. The disqualification of a large part of the educated immigrant population in societies which value education as a process of self-development is symptomatic of double standards. Labour market barriers to individuals' productivity carry consequences borne by the groups and individuals affected, and in the long run, by society.

At the individual level, Phillimore (2008, p.322) notes that those who feel that their skills and abilities are not valued or utilized effectively might easily 'internalize negative self-perceptions and develop feelings of alienation and worthlessness in relation to the local community and wider society. Such feelings would undoubtedly have an impact on their ability to integrate in the long term'. Phillimore (2008, p.308) states further that 'several variables have been identified which can affect that process negatively, for example the quality of a refugee's initial reception, racism and enforced dependency'.

Minority Youth at the Crossroads and Slanted Views on Integration

The main body of literature on refugee integration refers most frequently to, and is mainly understood in terms of its 'practical' or 'functional' aspects (Korac, 2003). A matter of high concern in today's immigration societies is youth unemployment and risk of marginalization. Under particular consideration here is the phenomenon as occurring in the case of migration youth. The non-integrated situation observed in migrant youth in several receiving countries is not purely a category 'of concern'. It is a whole system of action of which youth are a part. This section looks at some related perspectives of Barnes (2001), Sayad (1999), Parekh (2010) and Modood (2003).

Barnes (2001) study focused on resettled Vietnamese refugees' attachment to their original and subsequent homeland (Australia). The author states that the strength of resettled refugees' attachment to their country of residence will affect the amount of physical and emotional energy that they invest in social participation. Barnes (2001) notes that the types of policies and services which can promote social inclusion during resettlement, and hence build attachment and social participation, have been known for some time. The author's research findings have confirmed the need for these measures. They were highlighted in interviewees' responses as the removal of barriers to the achievement 410- 'of educational and career goals, provision of the means for overcoming language barriers, facilitating of family reunion, and combating racism.

Barnes (2001) observes that self-definition of social belonging to either country can change over time. The author says that the danger of resettlement countries not taking positive steps to promote the full social inclusion of people whom they accept as refugees is that this can lead to their withdrawing from emotional commitment to the resettlement country and declining efforts to engage socially with it. If refugees, and by extrapolation, immigrants perceive themselves to be socially excluded in the resettlement country they may continue to reside there but they might turn inwards and identify themselves in terms of their ethnic minority status (Barnes, 2001).

Minority youth who are born or have grown up in the settlement country of their parents have known no other homeland. When undergoing the experience of social exclusion on the grounds of their difference, societal indifference and discriminatory practices, it is clear that the sense of alienation must be intensified and grave. Castles and Davidson (2000) drew attention to the fact that this can lead to the racialization and ethnicization of social relations, which in turn leads to further experience of social exclusion for the particular group. 'The downward spiral of a vicious circle becomes established. Logical outcomes are that the ethnic group adopts an oppositional stance *vis-à-vis* the mainstream, and that ghettos develop' (Barnes, 2001, p.410). This has already taken place in some segments of the Vietnamese community in Australia (Ferguson, 1996).

Excerpts from Sayad's (1999) book, *The Suffering of the Immigrant*, are presented here. On the topic of the 'crimes' of immigration, Sayad (1999, p.286) writes that 'a sort of hyper-correction is required of the immigrant, especially one of lowly social condition'. Since he is socially and even morally suspect, he must above all reassure everyone as to his morality. Sayad (1999) observes that 'republican values' have become a centrally emphasized topic, and explains this as one way of denouncing what the social and political morality of French society regards as the deviant behaviour of Muslim immigrants. These immigrants, according to the author, are categorized by their wearing of veils to school, statutory discrimination against women and the political use of religion, which is referred to as fundamentalism. It should be pointed out the reference is being made to the second generation of immigrants, nationals of France.

The immigrant is conscious of the suspicion which weighs upon him. It is inescapable because he is confronted with it in every sphere of his life. He must allay it and ward it off constantly by demonstrating repeatedly his good faith and good will. Thus, despite himself, he is caught up in social struggles because they are indeed struggles over identity. He faces no choice other than that of exaggerating his identity in one way or another. Sayad (1999, p.286) explains that:

Making a virtue of necessity, and to a large extent because of the dominated position he occupies in the structure of symbolic power relations, the immigrant tends, no doubt rightly, to exaggerate each of the contradictory options he thinks he has chosen, whereas they have actually been forced upon him.

At times, even an immigrant who is at the bottom of the social hierarchy within the world of immigrants, must assume those stigmas which, in the eyes of public opinion, create the immigrant. 'He must therefore accept (with resignation or under protest, submissively or defiantly, or even provocatively) the dominant definition of his identity' (Sayad, 1999, p.286).

Modood's (2003) writing transfers us from an understanding of 'equality' in terms of individuals and cultural assimilation, to a politics of recognition. In other words, we move towards an understanding of 'equality' which encompasses public ethnicity. This perception of equality is liberating, since it means not having to hide or apologise for one's origins, family or community and requires that others show the due respect that is generally accorded to others. The public environment and attitudes adjust so that this heritage is not stifled or expected to diminish. Instead it is encouraged.

Modood (2003) presents two conceptions of equality. The first is the liberal response to difference – the right to assimilate to the majority/dominant culture in the public sphere, with difference tolerated in the private sphere. The second takes account of the new identity politics – the right to have one's difference (minority, ethnicity, and so on) recognized and supported in both the public and the private spheres.

Modood (2003) states that these two conceptions are not alternatives or mutually exclusive. Multiculturalism, in the true sense of the word, calls for both conceptions of equality to be accepted. The writer points out that the contemporary discussion of equal citizenship and its challenge to the earlier liberal version of equality, hinges on the distinction between the 'private' and the 'public'. Issues which earlier would have been viewed as private matters, now become sources of equality struggles. It is in this political and intellectual climate that Muslim assertiveness emerged in the domestic political arena. Modood (2003) argues that the distinctive concerns and the logic of the demands of Muslims mirrors those of other anti-racism and feminism groups which earlier sought equality. His 'politics of difference' approach is not discordant with Kivisto and Wahlbeck's (2013, p.2) account of multiculturalism, which says that 'rather than forging an expanded societal solidarity by overcoming diversity – as assimilation is generally seen as entailing – multicultural solidarity is achieved through the embrace of difference'.

On the question of identification, Parekh (2010) lays emphasis on the reciprocal nature of commitment and belonging. A citizen cannot be committed to the community unless in turn it is committed to him or her. Likewise it is not possible for a citizen to belong to the community unless it also belongs to him or her. The commitment of the political community is expressed in its structural arrangements, policies, conduct of public affairs, as well as in the way the community understands and defines itself implicitly and explicitly. Central to this are substantive social citizenship rights that include opportunities for individuals to participate, contribute to collective life, access life chances and pathways to self-development and self-actualization. Moreover in diverse societies, communities might be disadvantaged structurally or lack the capacities to access participation in the mainstream society and the opportunities located there. In the interest of social justice and the political community's need to foster a common sense of belonging, measures such as group-specific policies and services, culturally-sensitive or differentiated applications of policies and laws, support for minority institutions and prudent affirmative action initiatives, are in order.

Parekh (2010) differentiates between equal citizenship which is about status and rights (largely procedural and formal mechanisms), and belonging, which relates to acceptance, a feeling of being welcome, and a sense of identification. Furthermore individuals or groups might enjoy all the rights of citizenship but feel themselves as relative outsiders, as indeed do some groups of Afro-Caribbeans and Asians in Britain, Arabs in France and African Americans in the United States, to name a few.

The feeling of being fully a citizen yet an outsider to which Parekh (2010) refers, can occur alongside a formal rhetoric of equality. The quality of individuals' citizenship and their sense of commitment to the political community is eroded when they perceive themselves to be on outside of their society. The author traces the paradox of being fully a citizen and yet an outsider to the degrading ways which are used to refer to certain groups and other disrespectful ways of treating or defining minorities, as well as the reinforcement of these through institutional or other channels. Authors such as Mullaly (1997; 2002) have pointed out that institutional practices which are disrespectful to minorities and/or work to discriminate are often carried out by individuals who might be unaware of or unused to acknowledging the negative implications of routinized practices or formally and informally established procedures.

Parekh (2010) states that members of ostracized groups are in principle free to participate in its public life, but often refrain from doing so for fear of rejection or ridicule, or out of a deep feeling of alienation. Socially ostracizing mechanisms lead to conscious or unconscious internalization of a negative self-image, damaged self-esteem and the feeling of being alienated from the mainstream society. On the question of how minorities in degraded status might achieve social recognition and rectify misrecognition processes, Parekh (2010) argues that misrecognition is rectified only through the undertaking of a conscientious critique of the dominant culture and serious restructuring of the existing inequalities of economic and political power. The majority or dominant group hardly ever is willing to concede on these matters. Situations build up, proceeding to different forms of cultural and political contestation, and sometimes violence.

Since Parekh's (2010) article was written we have no shortage of examples of how unresolved or mismanaged challenges of multicultural incorporation evolve into situations that damage the communities and countries. Parekh's writing of a decade ago cited Muslim protest in Britain in the wake of the publication of Salman Rushdie's *The Satanic Verses*. 9/11 and Charlie Hebdo tragedies are recent examples which occupy social analysts, researchers and governments. The current outstanding task, as Parekh indicates, is for multicultural societies to exercise political wisdom and develop their capacities for anticipating, managing and responding to the new demands that arise in diverse societies. For this task it is not expedient to try to prolong the use of the tools and frames of the past when cultural and other types of homogeneity were more common to societies.

Phillips (2009, p.1) writes that 'debates about contemporary Islam and Muslims in the West have taken some understandably negative turns in the depressing atmosphere of the war on terror and its aftermath'. He argues that we have been preoccupied with problems but not enough with solutions. Phillips (2009) argues that many areas of interaction in everyday life give compelling evidence and reasons for challenging assumptions and assertions that have been made about Muslims in the West. Parekh (2010) calls for multicultural societies to exercise political wisdom and develop their capacities for anticipating, managing and responding to the new demands that arise in diverse societies.

Ramadan (2009, p.136) observes that Western citizens of Muslim faith, or Western Muslims, whether 'practicing or not, and accepting the secular framework – are settling down in Western society, becoming an integral part of it'. They are acquiring the skills for becoming intellectually, socially and politically autonomous. 'In a nutshell, they are Westerners and are developing a deep-seated sense of belonging to their respective societies' (Ramadan, 2009, p.136).

Chapter 5
Social Work Professional Capacity Building

In the dynamic arena of migration, social work plays a central part in immigrant settlement and integration. Social services for newcomers comprise the network of supportive services specially geared to facilitate immigrants' efforts to become integrated into the new environment. As part of the practical task of settling in, they must forge new institutional and social relations, find livelihoods and meaningful roles in the community and ways of realizing their personal and social responsibilities and aspirations.

Working in the migrant integration field illuminates dramatically how relevant the values, principles and thrusts of social work are for the promotion of human welfare and wellbeing among all groups of the society. The holistic perspective and intervention field of social work spans individuals' and families' life areas, stages and experience. Social work has the scope for making service responses across the settlement experience. Of unique significance is the fact that social work intervenes in those action and experience areas where individuals connect with the human, civil, and institutional environment into which they seek to become integrated fully and equally as valued and useful members. Continual capacity building for integration work is important for the profession. Fresh challenges and tasks in the field make of integration work a joint project of both social workers and immigrants.

The generic foundation of social work thus constitutes a substantial base for analysing, understanding and addressing the range of societal and individual challenges and strategy alternatives which belong to integration processes. Working with migrants draws the worker out of narrower specializations, ideologies, loyalties and views in order to grapple with the human and social variance in migration diversity. Immigrant groups are seeking to become locally emplaced. The quality, efficacy and long range outcome of this social interface and interaction process are critical for successful individual and family incorporation and no less for wider societal integration.

Initially focus is directed to 'functional' arrangements or links to education and training, the labour market, as well as health and housing. Although these constitute the basic requirement for settlement and the start of the integration process, a composite approach is called for in building the service response because all these measures are interrelated (Fyvie et al., 2003). Functional integration indicators (education, employment, housing, health) give a picture of the situation of migrants in relation to the general population, or how they are integrating on a functional level. These indicators cannot be looked at in isolation since it is in reality the interrelationships between indicators that will offer deeper understanding of incorporation dynamics (Fyvie et al., 2003). For example, when unemployment and social marginality from the mainstream co-occur in the first generation, this can in the long term have negative impact on childrens' educational achievement levels, their wellbeing and belonging in the society. The migrant first generation incorporation experience can be reflected in conditions of youth wellbeing in the next generation.

Settlement

Settlement challenges found to be common to immigrants and refugees in Canadian society include language barriers, role reversal in families, changes in socioeconomic status which are often related to underemployment, unfamiliarity with the educational system and having to cope with the loss of the extended family, a vital support system (Walsh, Este and Krieg, 2008). Some newcomers may face discrimination and racism, which may lead to limited employment and educational opportunities. As a result of the violence they have experienced or witnessed, refugees may suffer from posttraumatic stress disorders or other mental health disorders (Chambers and Canesan, 2005).

Integration means immigrants' ability to participate in all spheres of society as the way to solidify their membership and belonging in the national community. Structural inequalities and different forms of social resistance inhibit individuals' and groups' access to participation in economic and other critical areas of mainstream society. Social exclusion and excluding mechanisms surface in several chapters of this book because a large part of the challenging problem situations of immigrant clients are linked directly or indirectly to interrelated different types of exclusionary mechanisms and processes. Structural inequities trigger or underlie many problem conditions with which immigrants struggle to cope and which they fight to overcome. Some minorities face more discrimination and disrespect because majority society and/or other groups have not learned to relate to the particular types of 'difference' which they are perceived to represent. The processes of finding and shaping suitable patterns of relating socially and constructively can be taxing and enervating, especially for the groups who happen to be 'different', or to be in an environment where they are different. In social work we often meet the 'maturing' or 'mature' problem situation when individuals are at a loss to find the material or intangible resources for coping with or solving impasses that have built up.

When participation terms are more fair and more open in critical mainstream areas, the labour market in particular, this will free the way for newer citizens, as agents, to utilize to advantage that range of critical related resources, opportunities and statuses which do not exist outside of employment but follow in its wake to reinforce the linkages to many other areas of mainstream participation and belonging. Earned income from labour market participation enables individuals and families to be economically and socioeconomically independent and able to work toward the style of living which they value for the good of their families and themselves. Non-access to labour market participation means the unenviable status of 'enforced dependency', which is a common presenting problem situations in social work practice with immigrants. Dependency for most individuals curtails personal autonomy. It cannot be seen as a form of integration. This default outcome of enforced dependency is seldom explicitly acknowledged. Enforced dependency is quite often among immigrants a condition of lack of choices and barriers to their productivity.

Membership and participation in the mainstream brings status and strong civic roles. Highly valued by the surrounding society as well as by the settling immigrants is the symbolic capital of being in 'working life', contributing to and strengthening the society of settlement. In other words, mainstream participation brings the opportunity to be in interdependent societal relations, namely in strong relations of 'belonging'. This is the potential in immigrant integration.

Social Citizenship

No state, or welfare state, would define marginal participation as an official type of social citizenship. Prolonged or 'enforced dependency' in immigrant client groups is hardly synonymous with full citizenship. In these conditions, the groups concerned would be entitled to social rights to welfare, and political rights, but not able to realize in practice their civil rights to just terms of participation in the society. This could be a case of the state not considering itself 'obligated' to bring in the excluded (Silver, 1994). Lorenz (2006, p.9) has called for social citizenship, an essential frame in social policy, to occupy a more central place in social work practice. Thus the thrust of practice interventions would not be mainly toward resolving single problems at individual level, but toward promoting or reclaiming substantive citizenship rights and duties. This Lorenz (2006) sees as the substance of social integration.

The social citizenship approach is based on the idea that a rights-based structure can promote citizen wellbeing. It focuses on political, social and civil rights as the key facilitating instruments underpinning individual citizens' ability to exercise full membership through entitlement to access and participation across the spheres of social life in the society. Social citizenship can be seen as furnishing a structural matrix for charting the society's fields of action and participation. It is supposed to embody the potential expanse of citizenship, membership and belonging. Social citizenship has come under critique for not being sensitive or capable of addressing different forms of inequitable relations which occur in the society. Feminist critique has pointed out that the current model of social citizenship does not address equality of status in a satisfactory way, since it falls short of accounting for the status differences between men and women.

From the perspective of immigrant integration, social rights are valued guarantees of 'basic' rights to cover physiological needs which must be met. These enable individuals to pursue other goals relating to self-realization and shaping the life style and life course of their choice. The social citizenship model can indeed be seriously critiqued because it has often failed to deliver the articulated conditions of equity and social justice for newer groups coming into the society. Social rights to welfare and social security occupy much space in social citizenship policy and implementation. This can also feature in the arena of social work with migrants.

In the social citizenship model, economic rights cluster in the area of social security, monetary transfers and the basic safety net of income support or public assistance. There is no provision for rights to gainful employment. From a rights perspective then, blockage to employment might be seen as falling into the civil rights category, as an issue to be framed as one relating to fair terms of access to gainful employment. Effective equality mechanisms can address discriminatory blockages. Equality mechanisms can however be more tokenistic than actually functional. Official bodies for 'enforcing' equality practices are not effective without independent powers of investigation. In cases of blockages to access, private resettling individuals seldom have the economic and other resources to seek redress independently in the justice systems. They must attempt to work through these impasses as private persons on the ground. While the social citizenship model is potentially a powerful tool for promoting immigrant integration, if social rights are taken to constitute citizenship for immigrants, it will likely fall short of addressing the tougher, more critical challenges of integration. In using the social citizenship approach, social work would need to keep sight of all aspects of the model.

The manner of defining settlement challenges of access is important. If blockages to mainstream participation could be understood as technical in nature, this approach might be more efficient in some cases. For example, we can assume a policy to have been originally drawn up with 'equality' intent. Generally policies leave some room for flexibility and discretion since the contexts in which they are to be applied are not always uniform or constant. Thus policies can be and are used with different slants and emphases, which are in turn operationalized at the technical or practical level through local or institutional regulations, accepted practices and notions, convenient procedures, routines and so on. Through alteration of the policy interpretations or the manner of application nearer to the service implementation or delivery end, the desired or needed change in practices could be brought about without longer involved processes of policy change. This is one case in which 'incremental' policy change would be seen in an advantageous light.

It could also be that 'path dependency' influences decision-making. Sydow and Koch (2009, p.690) state that path dependency is often thought of as 'the mere existence of timeworn routines, cognitive rigidities, or structural inertia'. Rather it should be understood as a process in which decisions become historically conditioned or historically imprinted. Initiation of change or policy shift is difficult in processes influenced by path dependence, despite the possible mis-match between the old modes of response and new needs and challenges (such as those for promoting integration). When patterns, procedures and programme responses are set to go in certain given directions, another process of path-breaking intervention is needed.

The structural focus for social work is also approached from the idea of root causes. Social work puts emphasis on awareness of the root causes of clients' problem situations and whenever possible, using available intervention methods to address these situations. There are both facilitating and excluding structures and institutional practices in any settlement environment. Immigrants and practitioners alike would benefit from having a clear understanding of how these work in practice. On the basis of such knowledge, both parties would be able to assess their challenges accurately and be better able to steer integration efforts in an informed way.

There are some task areas which, if situated at the heart of practice with migrants, would put professional practice into the dynamic flow of integration work. Newer citizens form part of the wider citizenry but conventional action and organizational systems do not yield so easily to the need for adjustments to accommodate later groups. Societies were built with different blueprints and moulded in response to particular lives and needs of the citizenry at the time. Difficulty in making strategic and useful linkages with the surrounding society is almost a common denominator sapping individuals' integration efforts. The social work portfolio has great affinity with the field of integration. Some of the strategy and intervention modes which would be salient to practice in the integration field are:

- Building linkages outward in all directions into the society and areas into which immigrants seek to be integrated.
- working with this societal cross-section of actors – professional, lay, voluntary, market, corporate and civil society bodies – to create networks into which immigrant clients might tap.

- Working to bring institutions to alter their practices to accommodate and to foster inclusion of new and diverse population segments.
- watching' the media to protect the interests of the immigrant population.
- advocacy.

Lyons, Manion and Carlsen (2006, p.204) propose that interventions which would have increasing relevance in the international context of social work would 'include conflict resolution, advocacy, linking with civil movements and other resources, and conducting research'. We would however need to be able to rank and configure the priority areas in a way that would allow us to maximize the potential for positive outcomes of practice at both the client system and the societal levels.

Rodgers (2013, p.18) summed up the nature of structural approach to the field in the following succinct way:

It's not easy to think like a social worker. There are perspectives one has to acquire that makes the world forever more complicated.

The 'bi-focal' vision thing has a lot of weight. Once you acquire it, it becomes very difficult ever to look at things the same way again. Social work is about facilitating the challenges and strengths of little systems – like people – with the challenges and strengths of big systems – like communities, government, and countries.

In a study on refugee community organizations (RCOs) in Britain, Phillimore (2010, p.181) found that because of institutional constraints, and in spite of their having been specifically mandated to support newcomer integration, RCOs were 'functioning only with individuals rather than working with institutions to transform systems and ensure welfare provision is adapted to account for diverse needs'. Lundy (2004) emphasizes the importance of being aware of the ways in which personal troubles are lodged in broader social forces. The author states that by using a critical analysis approach in practice, social workers will be able to identify clearly the connection between the material reality (economic, social, political, legal) and personal or individual reality (self concept, emotional life, personal troubles) of those seeking assistance.

The societal perspective is thus a core element in migrant social work since integration is a process involving individuals' and families' becoming re-embedded in societal processes, transactions and networks in the new society. In consciously having a more comprehensive view of the spaces of engagement, we can make stronger functional linkages and alliances with diverse bodies and actors, thus expanding the potential resource base for promoting social integration.

Categories

In their work on the development of the human services, (Barnetz and Vardi (2014, p.83) state that even though institutions and organizations define the criteria for categorizing individuals in order to implement uniform treatment, 'It is clear that categorizing individuals does not change the fact that they remain distinct in their behavior, attributes, lifestyles, and needs'. This contradiction is intensified when the categories used in an organization to define their clients rely heavily on social stereotypes (race, ethnicity, cultural background, gender, age, position, for example) which are validated through their activities (Barnetz and Vardi, 2014; Thompson, 1998). Through the minimization of differences between people, bureaucratic organizations work to increase rather than minimize discrimination towards certain groups (Shenhav, 1999).

The positioning of social work in organized welfare means that areas of practice interventions are structured around a matrix of categories relating to different entitlements and intervention patterns. Understanding presenting scenarios of migrant clients' service and assistance needs requires the requisite contextual knowledge base on individual clients and groups of diverse backgrounds, experience and circumstances. This will help to reduce the risk that assessments, analyses and decisions on courses of action might become compromised if approaches are tied too directly or too closely into conventional strategy and intervention types.

Intervention styles which have proven their worth in particular national welfare contexts and prevailing culture-based value systems are not always or necessarily suitable to problem situations arising in settlement, especially in complex problem situations such as custody, marital or family break-up. The participation of migrant individuals and families in the shaping of interventions is critical. If necessary, other support and resource networks should also be involved. The shaping of effective migrant settlement and integration interventions will depend much on the input and collaboration of those undergoing transition experiences. The client or client families would need moreover to be able to participate in these processes in an informed manner, which requires that they have accurate insight into how the welfare system is working, being used to address the particular situation and what the consequences of different alternative course of action will be for their immediate and future life situation. This process aims at achieving mutual and clear understandings that bridge particular culture-based interpretations and expectations.

In practice with migrants, flexibility in decision-making on types and configurations of strategies will help to address specific situations. Additionally practitioners need to step back and re-hone strategies for addressing the specific generation of presenting settlement scenarios. Service responses will involve taking some distance from prevailing 'categories'/methods and keeping close to the generic principles and foundation values from which social work has derived its unique salience to human wellbeing. Appraising the suitability of conventional professional responses is an important part of professional and field development. New repertoires of professional service responses are being continually developed. It is one process that takes place simultaneously with professional practice among immigrant clients.

Cultural Dominance and Culturalization of the Debate

Critique of culturalization is not to try to deny the importance of categorization which in its generic sense, is fundamental to social organization. In our context here culturalization refers to the situation in which cultural categorical thinking displaces fair, more accurate and respectful ways of understanding people and groups whose backgrounds and life styles differ from what is generally familiar and what has come to be well understood and accepted as the 'norm'. According to Young (1990) cultural dominance refers to a situation in which a particular group's experiences, cultural expressions and history are held as being superior to the experiences and histories of all other groups. This idea of the superiority of one group's culture does not need to be articulated. By simply treating it as universal sets a cultural standard that puts others and members of other cultures at a disadvantage in the society (Young, 1990).

One facet of culturalization is cultural relativism. It refers to an understanding that individuals' actions, principles, beliefs and activities should be viewed predominantly in terms of their own culture. In another usage, cultural relativism is a crude means of adjudicating cultural difference, a custom of using the values of one culture to judge the *worth* of another. Cultural relativism invariably rests on superficial understanding of the systems of meanings that are held in other cultures. Ghorashi, Eriksen and Alghasi (2009) state that the main point in cultural relativism is that in a particular cultural setting certain traits are correct since they work well in that setting, while other traits are deemed wrong on the grounds that they clash painfully or are at variance with the particular cultural setting. They point out that the increasingly culturalist discourse in most European countries with regard to new migrants, is 'founded on a static and essentialist approach to culture, in which cultural content is considered the determining factor for all actions of individuals'.

Culturalization is disadvantageous in integration situations when it takes place at macro level. Categorical thinking using culture, religion or other markers brings about extensive stereotyping. When superimposed on social relations, it brings about societal divisiveness.

Ghorasi, Eriksen and Alghasi (2009) observe that in Islamic countries, and in immigrant receiving countries with Muslim groups, the perception of culture in others has been gravitating towards religion in the wake of September 11th attacks and violent events in Europe. According to these authors, the culture of migrants has come to represent a threat, which sentiment results in a social gap between migrants (including the second generation who were born in the new society) and the rest of society.

Resolution of the issue of cultural recognition has risen to be an urgent challenge on the agenda of receiving societies (UNDP Report of 2004). Ghorashi (2007) emphasizes that democratic culture necessitates the social recognition of cultural difference, since democracy is not solely about the majority, but it is especially about space for the minority within the polity. Stating that democracy is not only about people's liberty to vote, Ghorashi (2007) points out that space for the minority is what distinguishes a constitutional democracy from a populist one. In the latter, free rein is given to the voice of the majority without securing the voice of the minority. The author says that democracy without opposition cannot be thought of as democracy. In a democratic culture, democratic citizens are aware of their rights, yet they are also aware of their obligations to defend the right of the other to be different. Dogmatism does not fit into the democratic path, whether it be religious or secular (Ghorashi, 2007).

In the nineteenth- and early to mid twentieth centuries, perceptions of racial difference were important criteria in classifying and categorizing people. Culture has increasingly replaced it. The discourse features a 'new racism' based on perceptions of cultural difference rather than race (Stolcke, 1995). As discussed in Chapter 3, the culturalization of the migration discourse refers to a shift which sidestepped structural socioeconomic analyses based on class or race factors, to a milder level of debate that centres on cultural factors and a preoccupation with questions of identity and cultural difference. The multiculturalism model of integration was heavily criticized for diverting attention from hard issues of inequality and power imbalances by framing social relations in cultural terms. In the light of critique that model was subsequently modified (See Chapter 2). Culture can be used as a convenient device for explaining away issues which would otherwise require alteration of existing structures.

Advocacy

Lundy and van Wormer (2007, p.737) point out that 'Professional social work ethics and values require competence in policy advocacy and social change strategies, as well as a radical approach to individual, family and group practice'. This observation has relevance for migrant social work where the efficacy of integration efforts and processes can be promoted or obstructed by institutional practices in settlement society. Integration is recognized as a two way process in which much adaptation and learning must take place among newer citizens. Correspondingly the institutions of the receiving societies would need to be prepared to make appropriate modifications, or 'space', in their structures in order that newcomers will be able to join into the areas of participation and interaction which will lead to belonging and membership in the society.

Paul Loeb's (2010, p.10) book on social activism sets out an invitation:

> ... those who get involved view their place in the world very differently. They have learned specific lesions about approaching social change; that they don't need to wait for the perfect circumstances, the perfect cause, for the perfect level of knowledge to take a stand; that they can proceed step by step, so that they don't get overwhelmed before they start. They savor the journey of engagement and draw strength from its challenges. Taking the long view, they come to trust that the fruits of their efforts will ripple outward, in ways they can rarely anticipate.

Part of the mission of social advocacy is holding leaders accountable. van Soest (2012, p.106) has urged social workers to 'Hold yourself accountable for holding our leaders accountable'. Promoting social justice is not only the responsibility of particular professions or bodies. Young (2004, p.383) has argued that the responsibility for justice lies with all individuals and that we share responsibility for structural injustices which occur 'through ongoing and normally accepted institutional relations and actions'. The taking of political responsibility would often entail bringing into question what is generally considered normal and acceptable, in so far as it produces or reproduces injustice (Young, 2004, p.383). Young (1990) cites Murphy (2000) in explaining how responsibility would be carried. Every individual could not be called upon to assume the personal task of righting all wrongs, which would be unreasonable. Rather political justice would enjoin persons to work collaboratively to make better institutions (Murphy, 2000).

There are two main reasons why priority should be placed on advocacy in migrant social work. In the first place, there is not much solid knowledge in the society of the circumstances of immigration and immigrants. Neither are the implications of immigration widely understood in a balanced or positive way. Advocacy is one way of bringing to the policymaking community and the general public more accurate portrayals of matters related to the impact of cultural diversity, as well as informed analyses of challenging issues relating to immigration. From one perspective it is actually the responsibility of those with particular expertise or knowledge to engage in public education in societal matters and contribute to opportunities for general 'enlightenment' in the population. Hoefer (2010, p.161) says that 'social workers have, not only an ethical duty to know how to advocate well, but also a strong self-interest in being able to persuade decision makers'.

Social work can avail itself of unique stocks of practice knowledge which can provide the fuel for impelling arguments and discussion in advocacy processes. Secondly migrants themselves are often not in a position to take part in public discourse because of their initial unfamiliarity with the society, and also because of their lack of channels to do this. Moreover their voice or opinions are seldom elicited in policymaking processes which concern their own conditions in settlement.

Advocacy is one way of bringing back to the fore social work's mission to promote social justice. Lundy and van Wormer (2007, p.728) state that 'the social work profession can be proud of its heritage as the only helping profession imbued with social justice as its fundamental value and concern and a long commitment to peace and human rights'. At the same time, there has been concern over the need to for renewed focus on the social justice mission of the profession. Beresford and Croft (2004) warn that social work is not likely to develop a strong emancipatory aspect of practice unless much closer links and alliances are built with service users, their organizations and movements.

Rome, Hoechstetter, and Wolf-Branigin (2010, p.201) conducted a survey among National Association of Social Work (NASW) members to ascertain the degree to which social workers encourage their clients to engage in political action and policy change. The survey findings suggest that a small percentage do so, while uncertainties surround practitioners' perceptions of which behaviours in relations are and are not ethically defensible. The authors themselves argue that in professionals' efforts to be politically active, it would be important to reach out to a wider constituency in pursuit of social justice. They draw attention to the fact that the NASW Code of Ethics calls for social workers to advocate for social and economic justice and to promote informed participation by the public. At the same time, there is also strong emphasis on client empowerment. The authors propose that there is no better way to empower clients than enlisting them in the fight for social and economic justice. Rome, Hoechstetter, and Wolf-Branigin (2010) quote one of their social worker respondents as saying 'With our educated voice, and the voice of our clients, we could be a great force in the political arena—where it's needed most'. Advocacy needs to be emphasized strongly in social work training, especially in the area of migration social work.

The range of advocacy activities is very broad. An overview presented by Strier (2013, p.349) includes the following advocacy modes:

- public education, influencing public opinion, conducting research into problem interpretation and preferred solutions, mobilizing the public, setting agendas and designing policy, lobbying, monitoring policy, and election-related activity (Reid, 2000).
- grassroots lobbying, direct lobbying of government, collaborating with political groups (Nicholson-Crotty, 2007).
- administrative advocacy with the goal of influencing a governmental program or law through administrative means; program advocacy that aims to bring about change in organizational practice and improve quality of and service access for a specific population; issue advocacy organized around the mobilization of public opinion in support of a specific policy change; and legal advocacy using the court system to bring about social or policy change (McConnell, 2004).

More Empowering Categories for Newer Citizens

Categories of vulnerability are necessary when formulating official assessments to justify particular service response procedures. These are valuable in professional use, to emphasize the seriousness of situations of social vulnerability. In wider application to large groups of immigrants or refugees however, categories of vulnerability (which label has a tendency to persist) prove to be neither empowering nor beneficial to the individuals or groups to whom such labels are attached. Vulnerability categories can become conceptual traps which distort the image of immigrants or refugees in the society and can impact negatively on relations in the wider public sphere of society.

Eastmond (2011) found that Bosnian and other refugees admitted to Sweden in the 1990s were embedded in discourses of trauma and vulnerability. At a time when asylum and welfare had become highly politicized issues, the trauma discourse furnished much-needed legitimacy and was a justification for access in a stringent asylum regime, as well as for obtaining funds for 'rehabilitation'. However the adoption of 'vulnerability' as a form of categorization for reasons of strategy led to the ascription of images of disability to the entire group, and held lingering implications for later processes of inclusion. This categorization which was a neat fit into state organized ambitious 'rehabilitative' programmes for incorporating newcomers conflicted very sharply with refugees' own self-perceptions and aspirations 'to quickly rebuild their families and their welfare' (Eastmond, 2011, p.290).

The study findings showed that the informants were clearly convinced that work and recognition of their skills would have been the most important remedy in place of extensive and lengthy incorporation programmes. Highly tailored welfare and integration measures can problematize difference as a basis for intervention, and when refugees bear the 'traumatised victims of war' image, this is also a reinforcement of notions that refugees are somehow vulnerable and incomplete (Eastmond, 2011, p.290–91).

Studies have shown that immigrants would like to contribute in active roles to their settlement societies. Welfare system clienthood and economic dependence, if prolonged, will sap the positive energies of settling individuals. Individuals will be more motivated to identify with their settlement countries once they realize that they are making contributions to it. They will also be ascribed positive status by the others in the societies. Social work's integration portfolio is broad and inclusive. It can accommodate both short term responses as well as those that address immigrants' necessity of joining the socioeconomically active population. Clients make integration progress when they are able to move onward to assume societally productive roles and when they share with the surrounding society the recognition that they are indeed valued and value-adding members of the society.

Family Aspects

The family unit can face difficulty in becoming integrated into the settlement society if weak socioeconomic circumstances dominate settlement. As seen earlier, although the levels of aid in the safety nets of different societies vary, public assistance is usually set at a minimal level which requires of recipients resourcefulness in managing their budgets and life styles in scarcity. This would result in individuals, families and youth having less autonomy in choosing a style of managing, living and relating to the wider society. It can be argued that there is longitudinal risk of weak structural integration being carried over into the succeeding generation.

When the first generation has achieved solid membership in the society, they have a wider range of societal resources to facilitate the 'integration' of their children. Such resources would include networks and contacts ranging into the society, rounded insight into the social environment, wider experience with its systems, in addition to being able to be robust role models for youth. Segmented assimilation in the second generation can also be traced, at least in part, to weaker integration of the first generation. The side course of integration in the second generation can veer toward subcultures and damaging affiliations among which the recruitment of minority youth into religious fundamentalism is a very contemporary example of this.

In some ethnocultural communities the experience of employment and social marginality can be community wide (Valtonen, 1998). Part of the reason can be unbridged cultural distance, and perhaps socioeconomic structural backgrounds that are radically different from that of settlement society. Migrant youth marginalization is the outcome of a culmination of factors. However if the phenomenon is disaggregated, specific policy and practice interventions can be identified for addressing the issue at micro, meso and national level. For example, at the micro level, fostering linkages into networks which are seen as having real value and positive potential for their futures, would be one alternative. This would include mentoring relationships which help with settlement tasks. At the meso level, working for family integration would empower the family in its role of socialization. Civic participation can offer a chance to be involved in community activities and provide opportunities for cooperation in constructive projects. At the macro level, advocacy and participation in the political and public discourse also fit well into practice methods.

Caregiving Work Outside of Wage Employment

Today's migrants often have originated in countries outside Europe and in societies where caregiving over the life span and youth socialization are still mainly the responsibility of the family. In economically developed countries with comprehensive welfare systems, part of this family responsibility has been externalized in differing degrees to the state. Improved gender equality in some welfare states has been facilitated by women's increased participation in the labour market, and through the state's publicly organized childcare as a service response. For many migrant families this has been an emancipatory mechanism for women. In others the preference might be for mothers to retain responsibility for caring for their children instead of going out to work. It would not be in the best interests of families' integration to underestimate their own modes of caring by crowding out the informal caregiving roles which might be their first choice. In effect, if there is pressure for women to give up roles of informal caregiving involuntarily in order to be part of the formal work force, it has strong overtones of gender inequality.

Adults who are not in salaried employment are not well placed in the welfare system since social security entitlements are tied to earned income levels and contributions. This can exert subtle societal pressures on women who choose to do childcare at home. Welfare states are predicated on full employment, and draw their legitimacy from a base of solidarity. Citizens support the institution materially through taxes from earned income, and politically through concurring with its public mandate for welfare provision for the citizenry. Paid employment can become unwittingly imbued with civic legitimacy overtones.

In this context of settlement, we assume that individuals have a degree of autonomy in making choices of life styles, including choices concerning modes of caregiving and socialization. For settlement social work it is crucial to recognize the immigrant family as the prime caregiving and socializing institution for its members during the demanding adaptation and learning processes of integration. Indeed the immigrant family is charged with the responsibility for 'protecting' (being itself a major 'protective factor') as well as supporting its members. In Olwig's (2011, p.179) study of immigrant and refugee incorporation in Denmark, Sweden and Norway, this author found that 'family relations play a central role in immigrants' and refugees' establishment of a new life in the receiving societies, even though the welfare society takes on many of the social and economic functions of the family'.

Socialization of youth in collective cultures, is a process carried out through the combined efforts of the immediate and extended family, as well as by significant others in the community. In settlement societies, this responsibility rests with the adult/s in the nuclear family. The 'support systems' are missing. Many informal and formal mechanisms and inputs can lend support to the family. Social networks (immediate and wider), the immigrant community (if there is one), and human service workers are sources of support and other forms of assistance. It is of critical importance to nurture protective factors to assist youth to buffer the harsher social contingencies in becoming incorporated in a new society. This of course can be helped along in many quarters such as the school and intercultural social networks, but the primary responsibility must be held by family adults who themselves are usually facing integration challenges.

When there is risk of weakening family relations, the social work skills of mediation and education are valuable when shaped to the context. Parenting styles in receiving countries are very different and generally allow for greater 'freedom' for youth, which is often a cause of conflict or ongoing stress in families. Parenting and socialization skills for migrant parents in settlement contexts have not generally been developed in the social work portfolio. Developing a body of skills around youth socialization support would be a preventive approach with significance for several areas including child custody. It would, like other preventive work areas, have far-reaching positive downstream effects. The supporting, strengthening and enhancement of family functioning is well suited to the skills range of social work.

The individualization mode which is built into the structure of welfare state relations with citizens needs to be revisited in the light of some client problem situations. For example, in collective cultures the risks of marital breakup is moderated by many informal mechanisms of support, negotiation, mediation and compromise. This is very different from the practice in receiving societies where the relationship between personal autonomy, independence and responsibility is differently configured. Since immigrants' informal mechanisms for moderating family crises are weak in the settlement environment, holistic work approaches with family entities, inclusive perspectives on family and intergenerational relations can help with bridging integration transitions, and work toward preserving the family's strengths and functioning energies until the direction their integration process becomes more clear.

Incorporation Dynamics and Relations

Immigrants might not be able to access areas of formal participation until some time has elapsed and enabled them to establish networks into formal areas. This is usually a slow process for the majority of migrants. Exceptions are the case of individuals who might find helpful contacts or networks through involvement in, for example, sport, religion, or cultural pursuits which overlap with those of the majority society. In a way immigrants can remain 'invisible' for long periods in the society. Nevertheless there is activity and engagement, which entail deep processes of learning, adapting, analysing and interpreting the world around them. Because of having to study the new environment, immigrants can develop an analytic insight into contemporary social processes which might be lacking even in some of the native population.

Integration is usually understood from a functional perspective, and is also 'measured' using functional indicators such as housing, education and health. Immigrants make a heavy personal investment in settlement and integration, but this dimension of goal-focused activity is not readily taken into account formally. Integration indicators capture formal aspects of integration or non-integration. A fuller understanding of the quality and intensity of integration-oriented practices and processes in the private life sphere and in informal communities would give a more realistic idea of the volume of effort invested by settling persons and communities.

In new immigrant gateways, one of the unacknowledged (and often thankless) tasks of settlement is bringing in diversity, multicultural, cosmopolitan and transnational elements and changes into resistant environments. If there is a strong historic understanding of ethnocultural homogeneity in the society, the settlement experience is likely to be one of many decades of resistance. The contribution of immigrants in introducing ethnocultural diversity constitutes the start of cultural cross-fertilization processes which have invigorated all aspects of life in societies in history and in contemporary times. Cultural cross-fertilization is never a smooth process. Like all processes of social change, it can be predicted that conflict and tension will inevitably arise as part of evolving social and societal relations. The societal situations arising out of change, and even the sources of contention, can be addressed and negotiated not only reactively but proactively by shaping or mobilizing public policy measures of many types.

Different Perspectives on Welfare Systems and States

Social work can be located in the public, private or civil sectors of societies. In welfare states, the profession tends to be concentrated in the public sector. Migrant social work can accommodate to work environments in all three sectors, each of which has its own advantages and challenges. This section presents some findings of researchers on how welfare states are performing in the area of ethnic equality and integration. It is useful for social professionals to look at their immediate working environments and institutions from an external perspective. This can offer insights into dynamics that affect both practice and wider outcomes in the field. Additionally, comparative perspectives help to sharpen analyses of institutional practice systems.

Comprehensive welfare systems, including welfare states, have an infrastructure which can furnish a secure base for settlement and integration service and programmes. Funding might be a problem for the system as a whole, but being situated in the larger state structure provides some stability to programmes which is generally lacking in the private or civil society sectors.

Welfare states rest on a base of citizenry solidarity from which they derive legitimacy. They have had their share of critique. It is not easy to critique the welfare state which is often taken to be the essentialization of national solidarity and equality-emphasizing ideologies. Welfare systems and in particular welfare states represent a critical point of progress in many societies when the introduction of comprehensive social welfare meant that risks in sickness or disability, joblessness, penury and lack of income earning capacity in old age, would be cushioned by social security entitlements and not signify, as previously, the socioeconomic ruin of many households. Nevertheless welfare systems, their policy structures and practices need to be open to rigorous evaluation, feedback and change if they are to remain relevant, responsive and effective in meeting the changing character and patterns of need across population groups, including those of newer citizens.

Welfare systems are built to implement social rights. Unlike human rights which are inalienable and related to the inherent condition of humanity, social rights are more akin to economic entitlements arising from the possession of the status of citizenship in a particular polity. Moreover they have been very closely tied to wider economic conditions in the society. Welfare states came into being in periods of economic growth. Their principles and goals are to sustain the welfare and wellbeing of citizens, the basic blueprint of which is not set in stone, but very much related both to prevailing socioeconomic conditions and to political factors.

The 'rolling back' of entitlements in welfare regimes is a contentious issue even in states where the level of entitlements has been pitched at 'middle class' levels. Examples of welfare regimes with 'generous' levels of welfare include the Nordic countries of Sweden, Norway, Finland and Denmark. The tinkering with the welfare state has been a cause for great concern especially where these measures can damage basic security in households that are already weak socioeconomically. It is also a matter of concern when any change initiatives to established welfare provision arrangements are suspect or conflated with sabotage of hard earned social security. In this policy climate, incremental tinkering with policy is often the default course.

Developed welfare states have been lauded for their comprehensive range of benefits, social security and services. Positive features of welfare states relate to different degrees of 'generosity' of benefits, coverage over the life span, range of entitlement and service responses and varying configurations of these. Immigrant settlement and integration have posed challenges to welfare states. In Scandinavia, the apparatus of the welfare state as it is currently applied is questioned on whether it is an adequate instrument for addressing substantive equality and equity issues in the context of ethnocultural diversity.

Rudiger and Spencer (2003) has observed that the general conception is that in comprehensive welfare, universal needs are administered to by an impartial state apparatus through procedural measures. Across welfare regimes, each national model will vary as to policies, the quality of the policy implementation process, the outcomes on the ground, and the convergence or lack of it with individuals' own value-based pursuits in settlement. Policy and programme approaches are shaped and limited in many ways by the welfare regimes in which they exist (Rush and Keenan, 2014).

In her research on immigrant and refugee incorporation in the three Scandinavian countries of Denmark, Sweden and Norway, Olwig (2011) found that although there are differences in policies and ideologies, it is harder to detect differences in the actual treatment of and attitudes towards immigrants. Olwig (2011, p.179) suggested that this is due to 'parallel integration programmes based on strong similarity in the welfare systems and in cultural notions of equality in the three societies'. In her study of refugee integration in Sweden, Eastmond (2011, p.289) found that training and retraining periods were experienced by immigrants as frustrating and postponing employment, which was seen by them as the key to becoming integrated in the new society. The author observes that the emphasis on learning and changing resonate with the long tradition of Nordic welfare states. For the refugees, this also meant that they were involuntarily dependent on the welfare system. Eastmond (2011, p.289) states that:

Many of my informants, with a background of self-sufficient and often successful lives in Bosnia, resented the role of being clients in the welfare system and the dependency and control it entailed. Having to report to the welfare office regularly imposed limits on mobility and autonomy. It could also be humiliating.

Engebrigtsen (2007) studied integration processes among Tamil and Somali families in Norway. The findings suggest that strong government involvement in what in other countries are regarded as private social domains of intra-familial relations evolve into a state regime of different social policies and measures which amount to a compulsory system of resocialization that prepares migrants for the Norwegian labour market and society. The pressure which in practice is exerted on immigrants to adapt into prevailing mores and life styles of the majority society belie the formally declared policies of multiculturalism. Gullestad (2002, p.59) states that for Norwegians, immigrants represent a lesser threat as socioeconomic competitors, but more of a threat to 'the imagined moral community and the Norwegian welfare state as the incarnation of this community'. The author states that egalitarianism and equality appear to be tied to 'imagined sameness' in Norway. Gullestad (2002, p.47) writes that educated 'immigrants' often experience difficulties in obtaining employment that matches their educational level, and that it is common for 'non-Western immigrants' to be found working in unskilled and semiskilled occupations doing the jobs that 'Norwegians no longer want'.

In Pitkanen and Kouki's (2002, p.110) survey of the attitudes of Finnish authorities towards immigrants and immigration, it was found that while authorities have supported in principle efforts towards ethnic equality, the reality seems to be 'that they (and this includes employment agency personnel) would prefer to see immigrants in service occupations with low salaries and little social prestige (cleaning, driving taxis etc.). In fact, this is exactly what happens in Finland at the moment'. The main employers of newcomers are the industrial, cleaning, catering, and care services. Clarke (2009) states that projects which promote tolerance and placement in the workforce, more commonly in low-paid, temporary jobs, do not pursue equality. Pitkanen and Kouki (2002, p.112) further state that 'It seems rather difficult for immigrants to be employed on the basis of their professional skills and resources without any preceding work experience in Finland'. Writing in 2000, Forsander and Alitolppa-Niitamo made the observation that work experience gained abroad is seldom appreciated in Finland. Extensive underemployment of educated immigrants is symptomatic of blockages of their productivity.

Ahmed-Mohammed (2013, p.464) examines social work's relation to state welfare systems. The author notes that historically professional practice has based itself on institutional power for carrying out its functions and that 'the fact that social workers carry out their work in public bodies which are legitimized by society to promote general welfare, means that they have sufficient ethical reasons to not question their everyday professional practice'. This relationship is seen by the author to have inherent drawbacks, the chief of which are: the practice becoming bureaucratized, epistemological frameworks remaining static, and professional commitment being tied primarily to the institution in which social workers practice. Ahmed-Mohammed (2013, p.464) comments that in 'the framework of the public welfare bodies, these characteristics are interrelated and eventually lead to stagnation of the discipline and the profession'. He suggests that this can result in theoretical and practice proposals and initiatives alternative to those existing in the status quo simply being discounted. Far from suggesting that social work be developed outside of the state field, the author proposes that professional practice would derive benefit by opening up to alternative theories and intervention proposals and initiatives which are as legitimate as those that have already found their way into established practice.

Having previously been mainly a country of emigration, Italy is among the 'latecomers' which have more recently become immigrant receiving countries. Barberis and Boccagni (2014) speak of undeveloped immigrant policies, residually resourced immigrant integration service response, and a weakly institutionalised anti-discrimination culture as features characterizing the context of social work practice in Italy. The debate on oppression, discrimination and recognition of immigrant and ethnic minorities in social work training and research is still to be developed. Barberis and Boccagni (2014) see this as a 'dilemma between ethical universalism and tacit nativism that is inherent in practice with minority clients'. The authors also point to a tendency to overculturalize difference in both professional attitudes and in organizational routines. Nonetheless, in spite of the fact that the immigration experience of Italy is relatively short, Barberis and Boccagni (2014, p.83) draw attention to fact that although Italy is a new immigration country, 'the comparative significance of the Italian case, in terms both of social welfare policy and of social work practice' is clear.

Chapter 6
Challenges, Opportunities, Strengths

Introduction

Migration is a test of individuals' abilities and skills of engagement, perception, innovation, coping and endurance. Integration is a quest to find fields of productive engagement in a new society. Migration over national borders entails a degree of social uprooting as well as the prospect of entering new social, cultural and opportunity spheres. The interaction of newcomers and native populations sets in motion processes of mutuality which can be grasped as fresh chances for adding value to social life.

The necessary response to being separated from their networks is a conscious effort to rebuild compensating social networks in the new communities. Immigrants and their families can acquire a unique skill of reconstituting extended networks in settlement through making surrogate kinship and friendship relationships among persons in the surrounding communities, including the majority community. While it is not possible to replace original circles, social networks can be restored (Valtonen, 1994). Undergoing the experience of adapting to a new society is a process that enables the individuals involved to gain much insight into ways of accommodating difference and diversity in social relations.

Adaptation processes are often seen through the prism of 'culture'. Enculturation is defined as the process through which individuals develop the skills, knowledge, values and attitudes which enable them to become functioning members in their own society. They acquire a sense of the behavioural boundaries and correctness which prevail in social life. Acculturation on the other hand, refers to the acquisition and/or knowledge of the appropriate value orientations, behavioural modes and limits, as well as attitudes with which individuals must be familiar in order to function in a new society (see Kottak, 2005; Walsh, Este and Krieg, 2008).

When people immigrate they enter new localized systems of understandings. Learning to relate to these and to function in the contexts of local frames of understandings is part of the acculturation process. It is not always easy to adapt to the mores of the settlement society, but newcomers need to be aware of them and to appreciate their underlying 'logics' and origin. The increased diversity in societies changes the landscape and dynamics of cultural differences. The pressure to conform is gradually diffused, which in the long run, knits the plural society together with solidarity that is rooted also in cultural cross-fertilization.

Dealing with gaps between policy and practice or between the rhetoric and the reality are often part of social life for citizens. For newer citizens it takes some time to identify these gaps as they gradually become familiar with how things work in practice. Information on formal legislation and policies early in settlement is useful, but as individuals interface with institutions they begin to understand how society functions. Settling newcomers come to comprehend the society through experience, and possibly indirectly through the shared experience of those who have been settling longer as well as from contacts in the majority groups. In their ability to guide newcomers, settled immigrant communities can be a significant resource in facilitating and easing integration processes. A wide field of interaction allows settling immigrants to glean useful insights into the society, balanced perspectives on social relations and not least, valuable social contacts. Greater participation in public discourse would draw individuals into the public sphere to engage with discursive circles who are interested in exploring from various perspectives how social institutions and governments work as well as how they affect lives of citizens. The central ideals or guiding principles in settlement society need to be understood, as well as the way these ideals are realized in everyday life of citizens.

Equality and Inequality

In scrutinizing 'equality' it is important to distinguish between formal and substantive equality. Formal equality requires that law apply equally to all the people to whom it was designed to apply. Hughes (1999) explains that substantive equality is a type of equality which is satisfied only when policy or law is made meaningful for all members of society, including those who have been racialized or otherwise systemically defined by gender, sexuality, or disability or similar characteristics. A substantive approach to equality therefore guarantees not only equality before and under the law, but also equal benefit of the law. Substantive equality is the more appropriate foundation for equality goals since it embraces both the practice of equality and its outcomes (Hughes, 1999). Substantive equality is based on the understanding that meting out equal treatment to everyone does not necessarily lead to just outcomes.

Biles et al. (2012, p.89) states that formal equality tends to be focused upon traditionally in international comparisons because 'it is far simpler to ascertain what legal frameworks are in place'. The writer illustrates this using Canada as an example. Canadian scores on MIPEX Migrant Integration Policy Index show that it has established strong policies and legal frameworks for supporting the formal equality of immigrants. However in the specific areas of social integration its scores are not as strong.

Social citizenship has strong focus on equality. At one end of the equality spectrum, emphasis is on equal (identical) treatment of all citizens. At the other end of the spectrum the concept assumes a 'more radical meaning. It takes 'difference' into account, and interprets equality as requiring different (rather than the same) treatment (O'Brien, 2011). Thus at the substantive equality end of the spectrum, the failure to provide 'different' treatment is itself unequal because it does not address the unequal social and economic position of different groups. The question that arises is 'How does equality relate to diversity?' Diversity is not an alternative to equality, nor does it undermine the latter. When unequals are treated 'differently' in order to redress this asymmetry, diversity can validate equality. Evaluation of substantive equality conditions would be more useful than measuring levels of formal equality. Without measures of the state of substantive equality in immigrant integration conditions, it becomes easy for this to be conflated with formal equality.

Equality is closely related to fairness and social justice. In the context of poverty, social work and social justice, Craig (2002) defines social justice as a framework of political objectives which is pursued through social, economic, environmental and political policies. Social justice is based on the acceptance of difference and diversity, and on values concerned with achieving fairness and equality of outcomes and treatment. It recognizes the dignity and equal worth of individuals and encourages their self-esteem. Social justice is concerned with the meeting of basic needs, the reduction of inequalities in wealth, income and life chances and promotes the participation of all, including the most disadvantaged. Craig's (2002) thick definition of social justice puts weight on the substantive dimension of equality.

Ernst's (2012) study of the welfare rights movement in the US has relevance to this discussion on formal and substantive equality dynamics. The author draws attention to the decision-making styles in grassroots welfare rights organizations. The study findings demonstrate that even in the field of progressive activism, it is common for the organization and policy goal selection to be directed by professional paid organizers' perspectives over those of low-income activists in the organization. These decisions in turn have impact on whose voices are heard and whose are silenced.

Ernst (2012) states that 'cosmetic colorblindness' in organizational settings is the modern mechanism that brings about the systematic silencing of the voice of racial minorities. The actions and decision-making processes in welfare rights organizations are not always inclusive. Emst proposes a 'consciousness' framework that would incorporate multiple narratives, leading to the building of more inclusive policy agendas in the field of welfare rights activism. Ernst's work touches on substantive equality issues. The author draws attention to how equality in its thin version can be blind to the very forms of particular inequality which are being officially addressed. The author points to a 'deep need for a broader articulation of social justice' (Ernst, 2012, p.140).

Social Exclusion

In this discussion of social exclusion, the work of Hilary Silver (2007) is referred to for clarification and history of the concept. Social exclusion is understood to be a multidimensional process of progressive social rupture. Exclusion breaks the wider social bond holding groups together in the larger society. Groups and individuals become detached from social relations and institutions, and disengaged from fully participating in the normal, normatively prescribed activities of the society in which they live (see Silver and Miller, 2006; Silver, 1994). This can happen regardless of the formal status which they hold, for example, with respects to social rights.

In examining the dynamics of exclusion, focus should be on its two distinct parties, the excluders as well as the excluded. The effects of exclusion are experienced at micro and macro level. Different trajectories of group relations, interpersonal relations and institutional relations which are involved in social exclusion require that study of the problem include examination not only of those excluded but also the excluding institutions and individuals benefitting from the process (Silver, 2007).

The social exclusion concept originated in France which has the most extensive commitment to fighting social exclusion. It is articulated in legislation that deals with preventing and combating different types of social exclusions. A National Observatory for the Study of Social Exclusion is an institutional focal point for the country's thrust to effect its reduction in society. The social exclusion idea was adopted elsewhere, for example, in Britain and other EU countries. However it has remained a conceptual and policy approach that is used more frequently in European settings. Assimilation still is the foremost theoretical frame in the US, while multiculturalism prevails in Canada, Australia and other countries which exercise combined approaches to social integration. Assimilation and multicultural concepts have changed meaning gradually, as has happened in the case of social exclusion.

Silver (2007) states that the social exclusion concept has undergone change in the course of diffusion into different societal contexts. Exclusion was understood in France through the Republican lens of the social bond (lien social). In the EU the concept was broadened to include material disadvantage as well as social rights. Silver (2007) points out that social exclusion is *context-specific*. Thus national specificity in interpretation and reporting on exclusion indicators makes it necessary to shape context-dependent definitions of social belonging and the markers of what is considered to be full societal participation. The author states that the most expedient way of obtaining this information is to consult primary sources, the citizens themselves. This point would apply more widely to international comparative studies in general. Comparison of scores on common indicators which are ascribed differing national connotations and interpretations can be more of an exercise in quantification and less a valid portrayal of actualities.

At present social exclusion is scrutinized along a broad range of dimensions. In addition to economic and human capital (education, health) aspects, the concept can accommodate social and civic participation, non-monetary assets, citizenship, public services, political and civic engagement. Silver (2007) states that in Europe, researchers bring in the dimensions of poor future prospects, economic precariousness, multiple deprivation in depressed cities and regions, homelessness, housing and also access to the Internet.

In the present context of immigrants and refugee integration, 'bleak future prospects' is possibly the most socially and personally corrosive dimension in exclusion. It diminishes motivation to pursue settlement goals and forge bonds of social belonging. In the case of immigrant youth, the possibility of this type of exclusion should be a priority concern in the areas and locations where such risks are occurring. Silver's (2007) study on the case of Europe and Middle East youth turns focus to constructive social outlets beyond work and marriage for youth's energy and aspirations. Community based projects in the arts, new technologies, infrastructure, sports, and the environment are mentioned. Most importantly, the inclusion of 'the younger generation in the effort to improve its own societies may prove the most valuable development strategy there is' (Silver, 2007, p.39).

From another perspective Walsh, Este and Krieg (2008, p.902) describe social exclusion as a condition in societies when certain groups or individuals are unable to participate fully in the social life because of structural inequalities or barriers to access to social, economic, political and cultural resources. Such inequalities arise out of different forms of oppression on the basis of race, class, gender, disability, sexual orientation, immigrant status and background, as well as religion. Dodgsen and Struthers (2005, p.339) refer to 'the notion of vulnerability due to genetic, social, cultural and/or economic circumstances'.

Combating social exclusion calls for interventions of scale, and broader social and economic change in societies. O'Brien (2011, p.156) acknowledges the critical role of work at micro and meso levels in promoting social justice, but also emphasizes that 'A comprehensive approach to social exclusion requires much more systematic efforts to advance social justice through working for and towards social change'.

Social exclusion is examined by Castel (2000) along the two dimensions of insecure work and vulnerable relations. The author studies factors which are common across different vulnerable groups such as the jobless, people searching for employment and on training schemes, income support clients, lone mothers and economically destitute families. On the economic dimension, integration/non-integration through work is the relationship to the means by which individuals succeed or fail in reproducing their existence on an economic level. They are threatened by the insufficiency of material resources, and their state might be characterized in terms of lack (lack of earnings, adequate housing, medical care, education, and lack of power or of respect).

Castel (2000) points out that their circumstances are at the same time rendered more fragile by instability in the fabric of their social relationships. Along the social dimension, integration/non-integration into a social and family network, is the involvement in (or breakdown of) a system of relationships, through which existence on an emotional and social level can be reproduced. Individuals in insecure labour market relations will also face some level of material deprivation. A risk that can run parallel to marked vulnerability on the labour market is the possibility of greater fragility of social relations, which can lead to a process of disaffiliation, or weakening of the bond with society. Fragility of social and societal relationships can result in social isolation.

Castel's (2000) concept of disaffiliation reflects also the idea of social alienation when individuals or groups become socially and identificationally detached from the surrounding society. Isolation describes an individual state in relation to others, whereas in disaffiliation and alienation emphasis is on the social linkage, relationship or bond with the society and on its condition. As Silver (2007) noted, social exclusion includes micro as well as macro aspects. Castel (2000, p.34) states that 'Exclusion is not only an extreme state; it is the effect of a cumulative logic of deprivation (disaffiliation) which runs through wage society. In order to confront exclusion, it would be necessary to analyse back to the sources and processes which gave rise to it and which are still at work the society today.

Oppression

Young (1990) and Frye (1983) drew attention to oppression as a structural phenomenon that immobilizes, or reduces a group. Oppression was originally associated with the tyranny of a ruling group over subjected groups. Later understandings diffused responsibility for oppression. Instead of a ruling despot we see oppression as structural and created in the everyday practices of 'well-intentioned' liberal society. Young (1990) wrote that oppression is perpetrated through systemic constraints and are embedded in the unquestioned norms, habits and symbols, as well as in common assumptions on which institutional rules and practice come to be grounded. Since oppressions are systematically reproduced in economic, political and cultural institutions of mainstream society, it is unlikely that they will be eliminated through a change of rulers or new laws. In seeking to address oppression, there is no readily identifiable oppressing agent or group.

Young's (1990) observes that different strains of privilege and oppression exist in the conditions or circumstances of single individuals. This supports the need for a plural explication of the concept of oppression which is the only way to capture its varying facets. Distributive injustices, for instance, should not be equated with oppression, which involves a much wider spectrum of justice issues. On the other hand it is clear that fair and equitable distribution of goods is one aspect of justice. However for those having to be only and always, on the receiving end rather than as participants in the construction of the distribution itself, this is clearly an injustice. Young's (1990) observation is relevant to the situation among marginal groups, including immigrant groups, who can find themselves in enforced dependency on welfare states – on the receiving end.

Oppression shares with social exclusion the idea of a condition in groups which is the result of cumulative encounter with discriminating practices, norms, institutional or/and bureaucratic level mechanisms. Young's (1990) emphasis was very timely in bringing to the fore the idea of the unconscious reproduction of such practices by people carrying out routines but not engaging with the ultimate result or the ultimate societal and social consequences of 'normal' actions. Tilly (1998) elaborated on these mechanisms in terms of 'emulation' and 'adaptation' processes in organizations which promote embedding of oppressive elements in institutions and in wider society in general.

There is a comprehensive range of actions, interventions and processes which can counterbalance oppression. In the social work portfolio, advocacy, policy practice, inclusive social work practice, social activism and community development are some of the methods suitable in anti-oppressive practice. Anti-oppression action includes also taking 'political responsibility', a response elaborated by Young (2004), which is described in Chapter 5. Very relevant also is oppressed individuals' responsibility to resist their own oppression in Silvermint's (2013) discussion from a political philosophy perspective (presented in Chapter 3).

This overall understanding of oppression as a structural phenomenon is useful in shedding light on structural phenomena which relate to immigrant settlement and integration processes. Segregated patterns in residential locations, for example, focus on geographic clustering which might hinder integration with majority society. Boundary-making can occur around more desirable areas of opportunity. Enclosures refer to entities which occupy a protected space for retaining control over different types of social 'goods' and opportunities. As mentioned earlier, if the 'goods' in question are not private but public 'goods', such activity is a strain of misappropriation. These sub-structures all serve to impose limits on the societal participation space accessible to newcomers. In those settlement environments where effective mechanisms do not exist to combat such tendencies, oppression can be widespread.

Oppressive practices with systemic repercussions generally are the collective result of micro-level decision-making and other actions of individuals. These oppressive practices, it is argued here, can likewise be countered by micro-level individual efforts to reverse oppressive 'norms'. Oppression refers to systemic phenomena, implying the need for counter-action of similar scale and scope at various levels and in different contexts of the society. Oppressions, such as social exclusion, are contextual and take specific forms depending on their environmental setting. In the immigrant integration context, as a default option, the onus of addressing oppression should not be shifted to those upon whom oppression falls. In policy language, oppression is recognizable as a 'risk' area of settlement and integration. It would also need to be targeted by appropriate policies and effective measures as part of the policy agenda in receiving societies. The contextual nature of oppression means that contextual knowledge and familiarity with the particular oppression scenario would be vital in addressing it as a problem issue. Effective efforts for addressing and reducing oppression would need the crucial input and participation of actors inside the system that generates it.

Cultural encounter and the arrival of newer citizen groups in new gateways can give rise to resistance mechanisms in the employment market. A psychosocial catalyst for this phenomenon need not be fear of cultural difference, but rather a xenophobic reaction arising from the fear of displacement from secured organizational career paths, or fear of open competition for valued opportunity. In new and older immigrant gateway societies, protective mechanisms give rise to 'professional' discrimination – discrimination toward professionals *by* professionals, which in practice are barriers to productivity. Danso (2009) points out that structural barriers in the labour markets of developed countries exclude and deny immigrants access to occupations and jobs commensurate with their training and expertise. Moreover 'Denying people access to hiring opportunities for reasons unrelated to their abilities or industry is discriminatory, oppressive and unjust' (Danso, 2009, p.539). The high rates of chronic unemployment and underemployment among immigrant professionals can be seen as a meso-level screening out procedure practised in professional arenas. Precise understandings of equality-diluting phenomena are a prerequisite for addressing them. Resistance to greater substantive equality is a general occurrence in settlement environments. Acknowledging their existence is the first critical step toward shaping genuine responses.

The five faces of oppression identified in Young's (1990) classic work are exploitation, marginalization, powerlessness, cultural imperialism and violence. Marginalization is discussed in brief here because of its affinity with the social exclusion concept and its significance in present day integration contexts.

Economic marginalization signifies not only inability to take part in the productive activities of social cooperation but also weak access to the means of consumption. In the area of immigrant settlement, marginal status undermines integration in the sense that employment is a socioeconomic activity which functions as a springboard into other areas of participation which do not necessarily hinge on economic resources. As Young (1990, p.55) states, 'Most of our society's productive and recognized activities take place in contexts of organized social cooperation, and social structures and processes that close persons out of participation in such social cooperation are unjust'. ... The labour and human capital of marginalized persons and groups remains unutilized and non-commodified in terms of value.

In Sen's (1999) capabilities approach, this could be explained as the unbridged gap between individuals' employment related 'functionings' (capacities, acquired skills, experience, labour market potential) and their actual 'capabilities' (opportunities to use these in a useful, meaningful and rewarding way). It can also be seen through Maslow's (1943) frame of human need. The social welfare system might be a safety net that responds to material (physiological, shelter, security) needs but the critical 'higher order' needs for self-esteem and self-realization are for the majority mostly in the domains of education and employment. The 'life chances' of the marginalized are elusive since opportunities exist but in practice are out of reach. The policy question that keeps arising is 'What kind of position in the national opportunity structure is envisaged for immigrants?'

It is well known that not all working age individuals are employable. Some are not capable or not in a position to take formal employment. There is always a percentage who are inbetween jobs or on educational leave, for example. However, immigrant populations are in the main, young people. A great number bring skills, including professional skills, as well as employment experience which they have acquired previously. Others have been trained in the settlement country. Persisting disproportionally high unemployment rates among immigrant populations in many countries obviously speak of discriminatory processes. Moreover as Young (1990, p.54) states, 'even when material deprivation is somewhat mitigated by the welfare state, marginalization is unjust because it blocks the opportunity to exercise capacities in socially defined and recognized ways'.

Misinformation

Immigration and settlement issues are conveniently produced as election themes for populist parties. As indicated in Chapter 1, it is a common occurrence for populist parties to tip all societal discontents into the subject matter of immigration. This action taken at will in the political arena leads to immediate and long term social consequences which are borne not by the initiators of this activity but by immigrant groups. Weighty consequences include damage to majority-minority relations from the distortion of immigration issues and increased societal vulnerability of groups as well as affronts to their dignity as a routine part of the integration process. Selected perspectives are presented below on what Ungar (2008, p.301) terms 'the contradictory dynamics of the knowledge society'.

The following are perspectives from sociology and anthropology relating to misinformation and misrepresentation of immigration and integration issues. Ungar (2008) focuses on the persistence and intensification of ignorance in the ostensible knowledge society. In his work entitled 'Ignorance as an underidentified social problem', Ungar (2008, p.320) remarks that some sociological concepts should be accompanied by warning labels, and as an illustration, he states that the idea of a knowledge society is now 'so firmly entrenched that it is practically futile to try to dislodge it'.

It cannot be denied on the other hand that ignorance is firmly tethered to knowledge. In so far as knowledge is uncertain, contested and possibly permeated with ignorance, it is not possible to draw a sharp divide between knowledge and ignorance (Ungar, 2008). In the same vein, Dilley (2010) states that knowledge and ignorance cannot be considered simply in terms of an opposition through which the one is seen as the negation of the other. Rather the relationship must be understood as a dialectic between knowledge and ignorance which takes place in specific sets of social and political relations.

On the basis of his studies of the 'knowledge society', Ungar (2008) suggests that pockets of observed public knowledge – rather than ignorance – are the exception rather than the rule. Moreover while ignorance among individuals, organizations and even among experts is 'a serious social problem with potentially deadly consequences, ignorance remains relatively unrecognized' (Ungar, 2008, p.301). Ungar (2008) calls for emphasis to be put on the study of the cultural and institutional production of ignorance. This can be phrased as the processes of social actions or non-action which cultivate 'non-knowing'.

In a case study of the knowledge practices of Senegalese craftspeople and French colonial officers and administrators in West Africa, Dilley (2010) explores what an anthropological conception of ignorance might look like. We need not examine the case study here, but the discussion of knowledge and ignorance is useful especially with reference to intentionality in ignorance. The author states that knowledge in anthropological literature, is regarded as an unproblematic accumulation of what we claim to know about social relations, practices, cosmology, and the world. However, ignorance, the flip side of knowledge, is seldom considered.

Dilley (2010), utilizes the official *Oxford English Dictionary* definitions of the term to elucidate two types of ignorance. In the first instance, ignorance is a condition of being ignorant or a lack of specific or general knowledge. In the second instance ignorance is understood as wilful and intentioned. The latter understanding also carries the meaning of refusing to take notice of, not recognizing, disregarding intentionally, or leaving out of account. Thus in one sense, ignorance is about the limits to knowledge or the lack of knowing in some specific or general way. In the other sense it involves intentionality, or the conscious direction of attention in refusing to take notice. Dilley (2010, p.180) states that 'The latter sense of ignorance involving the intentionality of the actor places the analysis firmly in the political domain'. Dilley's (2010) argument implies follow-on processes of learning and the organizing of learning. This discussion leads us to focus in and to consider possibilities of practical engagement in the immigrant integration field. Tackling 'ignorance' in both meanings outlined above would be fundamental to efforts to reduce the negative social consequences for the immigrant and minority groups and individuals who are affected.

In the context of the EU, Spencer (2003a) writes that the EU has long recognized that integration is a central part of a comprehensive immigration and refugee strategy. Since migration will be a permanent part of Europe's future, an effective EU strategy will have to move beyond the provision of common minimum legal standards and information-sharing towards using to advantage the EU's unique position and role to promote integration. In a policy feature out of the Migration Policy Institute (MPI) on the challenges of integration in the EU, one of the priority strategies was on correcting misinformation. The strategy emphasized:

> Taking active responsibility for leading a balanced, informed, public debate about the reasons migrants are in Europe by putting into the public domain information about the contribution they make and barriers they experience, acknowledging public fears, and correcting misinformation (Spencer, 2003a).

Public Discourse as a Vehicle for Integration

The argument presented here is that the public discourse should be purposefully opened up to include newer citizens as an important participatory area for fostering understandings and sharing a societal vision with the larger body of citizens. The absence of immigrants from the forum of discourse that takes place in the public sphere of society is a longstanding and serious deficit in efforts to promote the social integration of newer citizens. This is related to their 'lack of voice', lack of recognition and their inability to be heard or taken seriously as persons knowledgeable about their very own conditions. Immigrants positioning as 'objects' is evident in policy and practice as well as in the fields of research. Wieviorka (2011) says that the time has finally come shift focus. He makes a call for serious consideration of the point of view of migrants as *subjects* in a global world.

The public sphere and forum of public discourse is a realm that is not much populated by newer citizens. It is possible that settlement tasks are the immediate concern of immigrants. Immigrant collectivities develop into organized activity as one of the outcomes of networking. Immigrant organizations take on the role of facilitating integration through many informal as well as formal mechanisms. It would be to advantage if linkages could be purposefully fostered into different planes of discourse in the public sphere. This is different from the strong ties and spontaneous dense interaction and communication taking place in informal communities in private life, or, in other words, in the private realm.

Calhoun (1999) defines discursive publics as groupings of individuals whose purpose it is to engage in discourse and expand their knowledge of the nature of social institutions and states. The 'public discourse' takes place in many circles, in many interest areas, and, even though unevenly, it is engaged in by a horizontal and *vertical cross section* of the population. It is a meeting place of diverse groups and a linking mechanism. The domain of 'publics' in the society, is a forum for collectively examining, rationalizing, critiquing, persuading, articulating, clarifying, generating insights, information and knowledge, with different cross-sections of the majority.

Immigrants' self-representation and agency in public life is an essential aspect of incorporation. British Arab activists groups who participated in Nagel and Staeheli's (2008, p.415) research defined integration 'as a dialogue between distinctive but equal groups sharing a given place'. The researchers comment on discourses of social cohesion that have arisen in the context of the importance of mainstream incorporation of immigrants. They point out that discourses should also take into account the sociopolitical dimensions, since integration is also 'a socio-political process by which dominant and subordinate groups negotiate the terms of social membership' (Nagel and Staeheli, 2008, p.415).

The inclusion of newer citizens into public discourse offers the possibility of mutual knowledge exchange across majority-minority groups. This in turn can reduce 'ignorance' or non-knowing among both majority and minority group individuals. Immigrants benefit from genuine insights into how the society works in actuality. These constitute a valuable integration resource. Furthermore discourse can lead to common understandings of the barriers to integration and of viable measures for addressing them. The information that is processed in public discourse can make a significant input into public and immigration policy decision-making.

The networking ties that are formed in the domain of public discourse resembles those which are termed 'weak ties' by Granovetter (1973), or 'bridging' ties by Iosophides (2007). Dense and close interaction is not characteristic of weak or bridging ties. Rather they can be seen as loosely linking, information-generating ties that allow individuals to make critical connections with persons in various positions in society. Public discourse spaces are generally open and in principle inclusive bodies which also would afford to newer citizens affiliation with a collective of similar interests. It would be a way to anchor immigrant communities into the wider society at levels of cooperation and shared discourse. Such interaction would have social and societal potential on many planes.

Chapter 7

Family and Caring – Transnational and Local

Introduction

The immigrant family can be understood as the cornerstone of settlement and incorporation. The immediate question arises over how the immigrant family will be defined against the backdrop of kin systems and extended family entities to which many of today's immigrants belong. In settlement countries the policy unit of the family is usually the nuclear unit, comprising parent/parents and children under 18 years. Migrants are not in a position to determine for themselves the members who constitute their family. For persons and groups from societies where close kin are also an integral part of the family unit, the nuclear family model can present the first adaptation hurdle.

The immigration policies in many receiving countries tend to limit their reunification arrangements to the nuclear family. Some of the traditional immigration countries such as the US and Canada allow a broader range of family members to be sponsored in as part of family migration policy. In societies without sponsorship arrangements, transnational marriage and nuclear family reunification generally are the channels for family class immigration. Kofman (2004, p.245) states that in European states the priority put on labour migration and the lack of official settlement immigration have been the main reasons for the neglect of family migration.

Transnational marriage currently is subject to more stringent rules and long waiting periods. Heightened precautions of immigration authorities relate to caution prompted by forced marriages. With respect to traditionally arranged marriages, Rudiger and Spencer (2003) state that it is necessary to be careful not to use migration controls to interfere with the legitimate right of women and men to exercise choice in the way they might wish to select a spouse. With respect to the elder parents of migrants, some states might allow the former to rejoin their children and grandchildren but only if these descendants are the sole relatives on whom they are dependent. Rudiger and Spencer (2003, p.17) makes the point that to 'have a family life and to be united with one's family members are not only human rights but preconditions for the successful integration of migrants'. Nonetheless the definition of 'family' is a policy matter.

Globalization has drawn societies into its dynamic flows of capital, services, information and goods. The human element, the people who operationalize these global or international processes, do not enjoy such free cross-border mobility. The exception to this is the small cosmopolitan class based on their possession of specialized expertise and experience needed in economic and technological centres.

The migrant family constitutes a prime resource in its members' adaptation and integration process. Intra-familial solidarity and the bonds between family members constitute a safety mechanism which buffers the demanding situations that form part of their settlement experience. Calhoun (2003, p.546) states that particularistic solidarities play an important part in individuals' lives and that it would be risky to undervalue the ways in which people might depend on ethnic, national, communal and other solidarities to solve practical problems that arise.

The solidarity within families is a vital support mechanism in the accommodation processes of settlement. The family not only provides practical help and comfort, but also constitutes a social environment where individuals can 'attain social recognition and assert their social identity in a foreign society' (Olwig, 2011, p.193). It is an anchor for social identity in new surroundings. Intra-familial solidarity has the innate feature of timelessness and continuity as compared with other solidarities which must undergo shifts with impinging changes in the wider environment. Social work in its role of supporting family functioning has a valuable springboard for promoting the social integration of its members. Much proactive work can be carried out to help individuals to work through settlement tasks effectively.

Olwig's (2011) three country study (Norway, Sweden and Denmark) of social incorporation in Scandinavia shows that although the welfare society takes on many of the social and economic functions of the family, family relations play a central role in immigrants' and refugees' establishment of a new life in these societies. The incorporation of immigrants and refugees into society is often viewed as being in the province of the welfare state. Olwig's (2011, p.192) research into the incorporation regimes in these welfare state societies led to the conclusion that approaching incorporation with the programme thrust of immersing refugees and immigrants 'in Scandinavian culture and society instead of as members of supportive family groups may have the opposite result of hindering rather than facilitating the sort of social incorporation that was intended'.

This finding has weighty implications for integration practice and practice approaches in welfare states in Scandinavia. The risk incurred is that of inadvertently undermining that critical base of family support which is an irreplaceable source of human empowerment in its members' quest to make meaningful lives in new surroundings.

Drawing attention to tightened restrictions in the policies and procedures relating to family reunification and transnational marriages Rudiger and Spencer (2003) point out that when immigrants do have their family with them, they tend to have a greater stake in settlement society. Instead of focusing primarily on remitting to look after their kin in homeland, they are motivated in a different way to participate in the society. Public policy and civic networks become increasingly relevant to them. Their concerns include, for example, schools, neighbourhoods and services for their children. They have greater incentive to put down roots in the environment.

Migrants' cross-border ties of kinship retain high significance and are one facet of their lives in a new society. Settlement does not bring with it a diminishing of ties with the country of origin. The concept of 'transnational families' is familiar in social research. Transnational families are defined as 'families that live some or most of the time separated from each other, yet hold together and create something that can be seen as a feeling of collective welfare and unity, namely "'familyhood", even across national borders' (Bryceson and Vuorela, 2002, p.18).

Separation and Parenthood

In migrant families, there is inevitably some level of separation from close kin. For differing reasons and due to different circumstances, migrants' and refugees' children, spouse, parents or other close relatives do not accompany or manage to accompany them to the destination country. Additionally many have kin and family in other destination countries. Migration, and in particular, forced migration separates families. Due to modern means of communication and travel, they maintain regular contact and often vibrant connections with dispersed kin. The expansion and affordability of electronic communication has enabled families to retain ties in a way which was not previously possible. In the case of refugees, however, instability and civic upheaval in their countries of origin can disrupt family and close social ties for considerable periods.

Caregiving across borders is another increasingly prominent aspect of migrant ties with homeland kin. It illustrates how cross-border family solidarity can work on the practical level. Kilkey and Merla (2014) charted care-giving arrangement in transnational families in order to capture the full range of caregiving arrangements engaged in by transnational families. Using data from a cross-national comparative analysis of Salvadoran migrants in Belgium and Polish migrants in the UK, the researchers developed a typology in which it is demonstrated that transnational families engage in proximate *as well as* transnational caregiving. Care flows are recognized also as being multidirectional and care relations multi-generational.

This study helps us to understand how transnational families retain their functional integrity in negotiating intervening distance in different ways. For example, remittances constitute economic or income support which is a central aspect in family responsibility. The flows of remittances between migrant communities and kin in the countries of origin are of a scale to make a critical difference not only to the lives of kin, but also even to the development processes in migrants' homelands. Caregiving over borders allows migrants to participate actively in their ongoing caregiving roles.

The four types of involvement in care provision, which were identified in Kilkey and Merla's (2014) study are: direct provision with physical co-presence, facilitated by visits, extended stays in either the homeland or settlement country; direct provision at a distance, which is facilitated through use of communication technologies; coordination of caring, or organizing a particular type of support; and delegation of support to a third person (relative, friend or carer), generally with regular information exchange on the caring situation.

Caregiving arrangements are very much influenced by the point at which individuals are in their personal, familial or professional life cycle. Relationships and negotiated commitments and, not least, the transnational family networks also play a key role in helping migrant family members to maintain family solidarity and overcome institutional obstacles to caregiving. Kilkey and Merla's (2014) analytic framework offers a more comprehensive picture of the range of persons and resources which are mobilized to effect transnational caregiving. The generally narrow conceptualization of the family in official policies tends to externalize problems generated by caring at a distance.

Local Parenting

In working with migrants an emphasis on the value of family is central. In recent times migrants come increasingly from cultures which have not shifted to individualistic norms in social life. In western societies the modern family is often seen as having a central value of individualism which downplays the importance of the family as a unit. The concept of 'familism' refers to core values of a family type which emphasize commitment to the family as a unit. Depending on context, it tends at times to carry a bourgeois image as well as negative connotations of authoritarianism and oppressiveness in relations. However, as explained below, familism also is based on mutual respect between family members and different generations (Mogro-Wilson, 2013). The societies of origin of a large part of migrant families are in the main family-oriented, and have not undergone the particular socioeconomic and policy changes which have generated 'individualism' as a principle of social organization and administration in many immigration societies.

Migrant family strength lies in its members and in its intrinsic integrity as a unit. The family is also collectively responsive to individual needs, crises, and eventualities. When the family becomes split or separated from some of its members, there is a setback which requires adaptation processes such as role substitution and change among members. Many migrant families have undergone or are going through processes of adjustment to their changed composition. Human services should be very wary of measures which might lead to further fragmentation of the family unit.

Human services and welfare systems in receiving countries are administratively structured to include individualistic interventions and strategies in their response range. Migrant social work would call for the repertoire of family unit oriented strategies and methods to be developed. It also follows that suitable support services targeting parents and caregivers in migrant families would be invaluable in maximizing family functioning in the face of settlement and integration tasks. The benefits of supportive measures for parents and caregivers would also be realized in the area of youth settlement and adaptation to the new social environment.

Motherhood in immigrant families can undergo a radical change in those welfare settings where womens' equal labour market participation is a key element in the structure of the social security system. The choice to remain outside of salaried employment is economically penalizing because individuals are then limited to receiving minimal flat-rate benefits. Ernst (2010) refers to the paradoxical situation when public sphere wage work becomes conflated with womens' moral worth. As a result the value of domestic work and motherhood among low-income women becomes marginalized. The narrow social debate over welfare dependency is one reason why Ernst (2010) makes a strong case for a broader articulation of social justice.

The values, principles and practices of parenting in different societies and cultures vary. There are also areas of deep commonality. The research on features of good parenting practices which occur across cultures and societies is scant. However we can obtain understanding of cross-cultural parenting elements through the perusal of country-focused studies. Mogro-Wilson (2011; 2013), who studied Latino populations, calls for social workers to be aware of cultural beliefs and values of Puerto Rican families and how they are applied to the socialization of Puerto Rican children. The author draws our attention to the need for seeking clearer understanding of fundamental culturally-grounded concepts as well as of culture-derived protective mechanisms in families in order to enhance the effectiveness of social work services and to increase cultural knowledge in the areas of policy, research, and practice.

Mogro-Wilson's study (2011) offers a conceptual model based on a combination of cultural, community, family, and individual factors which produce protective resilience-building mechanisms inherent to the Latino community. It describes how resilience factors for Latinos can be used by professionals. Her study was directed to building resilience among Latino children and families with disabilities. A subsequent study by Mogro-Wilson (2013) focuses on Puerto Ricans who are one of the largest Latino subgroups in the United States. The article presents a model for understanding how parenting is influenced by cultural values and beliefs. It is proposed as a parenting model for social workers helping Puerto Rican families and is grounded in cultural constructs. The model also provides specific guidelines for assessments and interventions. Constructed on essential elements of Latino culture, it demonstrates how parenting practices for Puerto Rican families are actualized through the lens of *familismo, respecto, simpatia*, and *personalismo*. These concepts are briefly discussed here as one dimension of multicultural parenthood in settlement environments.

Familismo can be defined as a belief system that refers to 'feelings of loyalty, reciprocity, and solidarity towards members of the family, as well as to the notion of the family as an extension of self' (Cortes, 1995, p.249). As Mogro-Wilson (2013) observes, the focus of family life is often not on the youth or child but on the family system.

Respecto, or proper demeanour, refers to adherence to authority.[1] Respect is consistently prioritized in Puerto Rican mothers' beliefs regarding desirable long-term socialization goals and child behaviour. This finding held across socioeconomic strata both on the island and on the mainland. Traditionally Puerto Rican families have been considered to exhibit an authoritarian style of parenting that utilizes high levels of control. Children are expected to follow orders, respect parents, and behave.[2] Mogro-Wilson proposes that parental control can be viewed more accurately through the lens of *respecto*, where children have been raised to respect their parents, and parents also respect their children.

Simpatia refers to a behavioural gravitation toward interpersonal harmony and avoidance confrontation. Simpatia is often viewed as a non-confrontational style which is positively regarded. 'Someone who is *simpatico* is willing to lose an argument, time, and other things during interpersonal conflict to retain internal satisfaction and affection-laden, smooth interpersonal contact, especially with significant others and within the family' (Mogro-Wilson, 2013, p.237).

Personalismo is a value based on trust, warmth, and respect in interpersonal interactions with others. In parenting *personalismo* is often thought of in terms of the development of strong parent–youth relationships featuring trust, getting along together, and making joint decisions (Mogro-Wilson, 2008; 2013).

---

1 See Harwood et al. (1996).
2 Fontes (2002).

Differences between parenting styles of migrants need not be viewed as directly conflicting with styles prevailing in settlement societies. At base, parenting is about equipping youth with personal and social resources, and skills for life in private and public spheres. It would be possible to identify common thrusts across cultural modes of parenting and to work with migrant parents in their socialization tasks, while at the same time, respecting the particular parenting emphases that have served their own communities over time.

From Collective to Individualist

In many migrants' countries of origin, caring and socialization are not in the area of public social services, but are a shared responsibility in traditional networks of kin and close circles. Arrangements in developed welfare systems differ greatly from those in less interventive states. As families shift from cultures of collectivist caregiving and socialization practices, this change is experienced in various ways. The shift depends on the difference between their practices and arrangements in previous family and societal contexts, and the way that the principle of individualism shapes policy, practice and social life in settlement. A common factor across different settlement scenarios is that the responsibility for caregiving and youth socialization becomes more concentrated on parents. In receiving societies where family immigration is more liberal and allows for sponsorship of relatives, this transition can be much less abrupt. This is not to say that parents abdicate their responsibility in collectivist cultures. Rather it means that other adult kin can take meaningful roles or form significant personal attachments with young people, all of which contribute to the fabric of social support. It is important to take this dimension of integration into account.

Socialization involves the development of protective factors which constitute an arsenal of dispositions, behaviours, attributes, skills, personal and social assets which can guide youth to encounter and deal effectively with challenging situations in social life. These factors also play a part in individual coping processes and in taking proactive courses of action to avoid occurrences of adversity. Some protective factors are especially relevant for sociocultural adaptation and integration.

Social support relates to collective life, association with close family, kin, friends, mates, neighbours and others with whom one interacts either occasionally or in daily life. For youth this would include classmates, teachers and other elders, for example, from religious congregations or community organizations. The concept of social embeddedness relates to the extensiveness or structure of the formal and/or informal support network of any individual. Finch et al. (1999) make an interesting point that the support one receives from others includes perceptions of the *availability* of support as well as satisfaction with perceived available support. Moreover since social support serves a host of different functions, both received and perceived support take on multidimensional aspects. We can direct our gaze to an individual's perception of available support from the wider society, the society of settlement.

In an environment which is perceived by an individual migrant as having, for example, racist or hostile anti-immigrant attitudes, the perception of available support might be weak. Moreover it would be a perception of negative social relations as well as a perception of lack of available support. Negative relations in the social environment constitute one of the integration risks that can alienate migrants and undermine integration processes and rooting. This is one of the harms against which youth would need to develop protective mechanisms if they are to take up their place and membership of the society. A social climate that is perceived as supportive of immigrants and their contribution would be highly instrumental in fostering newer citizens identification with the society.

Family relationships are considered to be a fundamental social resource which is essential for supporting individuals throughout their life course. Prandini (2007; 2014) states that family (i.e., primary) bonds originally converged with the idea of social capital in that both represented networks of interpersonal trust and reciprocity. James Coleman (1988) drew attention early to the family as a form of social capital. The family's social capital was defined as the relationships between parents, children and other relatives living in the same household. According to Coleman (1988), the family's social capital had a central role in building the younger generation's educational achievement and human capital. Subsequently, when the concept of social capital came to occupy sociological discourse in the late 1980s, 'family resources became invisible in mainstream social capital theories' (Prandini, 2014, p.222).

In a migrant integration context, the idea of family as social capital would have contemporary significance as a frame for understanding family relationships as an asset in youth socialization and human capital formation. Social capital as a protective mechanism can also refer to individuals' networks of relationships in the wider society. It embodies the latent and actual resources lodged in social relations and activated in understandings of reciprocity, mutuality and trust. Social capital has close affinity with perceived support and its availability. The reciprocity in social capital is often pliant, as exchanges can take place within a broad rather than restricted time frame.

Resilience

Resilience can be explained simply as a child or youth's ability to withstand stress and overcome difficulties, or as positive adaptation despite exposure to significant risk or adversity (Luthar, 2003). According to Kirby and Fraser

(1997) resilience can be understood as a personal characteristic or personality trait. As a personality trait, it would comprise a range of characteristics which youth manage to develop successfully despite growing up in disadvantaged conditions. However these authors prefer a more comprehensive understanding of resilience which would represent it as sets of competencies in dealing with threats to wellbeing, or as a series of coping strategies that assist positive functioning (See also Ungar, 2008). Resilience researchers further recognize that combinations of protective and vulnerability factors in a youth's environment help to determine how individual resilience is developed. These factors have been found to relate, in the main, to personal attributes of the youth, family-based characteristics and conditions, impinging factors from the wider social environment (Wu, Tsang and Ming, 2014).

Wu, Tsang and Ming (2014) conducted a study among 806 migrant children in Beijing, China, to investigate how community social capital, family social support, and children's resilience influenced multiple educational outcomes of Chinese migrant children. Higher levels of community social capital and family social support were both associated with higher levels of resilience, which in turn led to increased academic effort, higher educational aspiration, and decreased possibility of dropping out in the near future. The researchers state that their findings support the proposition of the study that protective factors in social contexts can be linked to the resilience of youth and children as a personal trait. They propose that particularly for migrant children in China, because of their marginal status in the urban community, family is likely to be the most important, if not the sole, source of social support when they have instrumental or emotional needs. According to the researchers, family social support is presumably the most influential factor in the range of social determinants of children's development. The findings in this study that family support might be the foremost factor in resilience development in youth would have wide relevance to contemporary scenarios of immigrant youth and family integration.

We can propose here that in the case of migrant youth, resilience would mean developed robustness and skill for coping with challenging settlement tasks and adjustments, and for overcoming negative social environment-based phenomena such as anti-immigrant attitudes, and possible confrontational situations. Family support networks and other sources of social support in the interaction and living environment of individuals are critical in resilience-building processes.

Coping can be understood as involving the strategies of cognitive or internal coping, the use of social support and purposive problem-solving to rectify the problem situation. In cognitive, emotion-focused or internal coping, the individual does not seek to change the situation, or indeed might not be a position to do so because of circumstances such as, for example, the overwhelming odds against such an attempt being successful. The individual comes to terms with the situation and the focus in on managing distress. Cognitive re-structuring, positive comparisons, consolatory cognitions, denial and avoidance, are among the strategies that can be employed (See Lazarus and Folkman, 1984; Snyder, 1999).

Social support methods, as described above, look outwardly to social networks and the surrounding social environment. In purposive problem-solving the individual sets out for concrete engagement with the problem. The aim is to create a solution, to seek change, or to contain or prevent the problem from escalating. This generally involves different sets of skills (interpersonal, group, communication, political, for example) which must be learned or deployed. Individuals who take this course of action estimate that they possess or can access the appropriate personal or social resources. Skill in situation assessment or appraisal, and previous experience in problem-solving are some of the person-based characteristics which underpin purposive problem-solving.

Prejudice and Racism

> I asked Horace what it was he liked so much about Valois … he went on to say, 'Then, of course, I get a chance to associate with whites on a social level. I can come to Valois and for a few minutes I can pretend that I am in a nonracist world. Valois is a special place on the planet earth. It is the only place that I have this much unity going on in my life'. (Duneier, 1992, p.115)

In the above quotation, sociologist Michell Duneier (1992) describes his conversation with one of the local men at Valois, a cafeteria serving home-style food cuisine on Chicago's South Side, which is frequented by a black and white male clientele. Duneier (1992) spent four years on his sociological study of an environment in which human relationships outshone race.

Racism is a part of life for many. In its different guises it affects individuals and whole groups in society. Prejudice and discrimination exist alongside each other in racism, and these take the form of actions, and covert or formal social, political or institutional practices. Systemic racism refers to the pervasiveness of this trait in many areas of society. Racism might be an individual-level disposition or the everyday practice of different classes or social aggregates. It is essentially a form of oppression.

Racism can be personally internalized by individuals who experience it. It tends to generate ascribed identities which over time can be corrosive of individuals' self-perception and self-esteem, especially when it is not counteracted by supportive and protective mechanisms. In the long run there is a high risk of social alienation. Young people growing up in an environment with racism should be focused upon for effective support programmes that would complement intra-familial and other support sources. It would be important for the society itself to reach out by formally acknowledging the existence of the problem and making a social investment to combat negative effects on youth and to ensure that the potential of the society's youth is realized.

The conventional 'tolerance' thrust might be turned around to build 'enlightened', tolerant and more confident attitudes' among minority youth themselves. It would be important for the aetiology of racist attitudes and behaviours to be understood by immigrant youth and the wider society. For immigrants, their families and children, this would constitute a cognitive tool for managing or coping in an oppressive environment. Such efforts serve to *complement* substantive and effectively implemented antiracist and anti-discrimination policies.

One of the factors which can directly promote alienation among minority youth is discrimination. Covert discrimination is often elusive, taking place as it does within and not outside the rigidities of laws and policies. Youth's frame of reference is emergent and plastic. If individuals begin to realize from an early stage, that the wider opportunity structure is off bounds, and that equality amounts in practice to a group-specific principle, then disaffection, alienation and hostility are reflex reactions. It is part of a paradoxical situation in societies when formal or procedural equality is allowed to be confused with equity. The case of their parents is often different because first generation migrants' experience span is lengthier, spanning complexities of personal and social changes which moderate their outlook on life.

Capabilities

The 'capabilities' approach is a useful tool for grappling with elusive phenomena related to social exclusion, marginalization and discrimination. It provides a frame for uncovering the kind of significance that exclusionary phenomena hold for affected individuals, and can shed light on the state of minorities' civic freedoms in the society. As mentioned in Chapter 4, functionings refer to ways of being or doing which an individual values highly. These range from being free from hunger or sickness, to the ability to be skilled in a certain area, to be able to contribute to community life, and be respected and in meaningful interdependence with the society (Sen, 1999). 'Capabilities' refer to the alternative configurations of functionings that are feasible for an individual to achieve. Sen (1999, p.75) says that 'Capability is thus a kind of freedom: the substantive freedom to achieve alternative functioning combinations (or less formally put, the freedom to achieve various lifestyles)'. Capabilities or the capability set reflect the freedom to achieve, operationalize or actualize alternative combinations of functionings which might be chosen and valued by the individual.

In the context of migrant youth, it is argued here that unreasonable or unbreachable gaps between an youth's 'functionings' or achievements and his or her actual 'capabilities' would comprise a grave and persisting obstacle to 'national belonging'. Although the 'capabilities' approach is not elaborated into specificities of contexts or cases, it can still be adapted to contexts. It would be important to take into account the nature of functionings. These often refer to skills or capacities that have been attained through effort on the part of individuals. Thus when individuals or groups are outside of the opportunity networks to realize or fulfil the aim of such efforts and aspirations, this brings to the fore core issues relating to civic rights, freedoms and autonomy of individuals. In affluent societies gaps between the functionings and capabilities of different groups in society tell of asymmetries in resources, opportunities, wellbeing and quality of life. Such gaps are not sustainable in the long run as they drive divisions into the society.

The field of civic engagement has become an active one in recent years. It comprises programmes which seek to engage young people to be active citizens, including research as well as evaluation studies. The thrusts of the projects include seeking to identify what kinds of programmes or strategies would enhance youth engagement in the civic arena. Applying the 'capabilities' frame for analysis, Levine (2011) states that the best initiatives, from this perspective, are the ones that achieve efficient and reliable improvements in tangible human welfare by enhancing people's autonomy. These projects 'do not manipulate youth but assist them in developing their autonomy' (Levine, 2011, p.18).[3]

Welfare of the Elderly of Immigrant Background

The socioeconomic situation of elderly immigrants reflects the 'conditions in which they have lived and worked' (Bolzman, 2012, p.109). The working life of the majority of immigrants tends to have been in the less well-paid areas of the labour market. In many of the settlement countries, the level of old age security is tied quite closely to the level and time span of income earning. Individuals' labour market history affects their economic security in old age. Immigrant elderly are generally overrepresented in the more marginal areas of the social security system.

In immigrant families cultural caregiving practices often are based on retaining caring responsibility within the family, as far as possible. Institutional care in its many forms, responds to care needs when families' caring capacities

---

3   See Levine (2011) for description of youth civic engagement programmes.

become inadequate for the age-related problems of their elderly parents or relatives. Culturally supportive institutional care arrangements for elderly immigrants tend not to be a high priority in the elderly caring sector, in the face of otherwise increasing ageing populations. The challenge is not necessarily one of financial resources, but rather of revisiting policies to make them more inclusive of the diversity which is now visible among the national elderly populations. Appropriate care for the culturally diverse elderly is a quality of life question which needs attention at this time. It is difficult for the elderly themselves to advocate for suitable conditions of care. The responsibility for working towards this rests with professionals in the caring professions, families and communities.

Transnational Families

Transnational families have been discussed above in connection with caregiving arrangements across borders. Since settling persons increasingly invest effort into transnational family life as one aspect of settlement and integration, this will come to be reflected in social work practice with migrants. Although geographic separation leads to change and adjustment in how relations are maintained in today's transnational families, when compared to the pre-electronic communication era, families are far better able than before to retain active connections and to carry out mutual assisting as well as other collective and social initiatives.

Many adjustments come in the wake of family separation through migration to distant destinations. Migration of family members is often, and has been throughout history, a strategy for families to diversity their livelihoods (Agoumi and Tamim, 2009). Such undertakings can be carefully and collectively planned, or can come about through the spontaneous decision of individuals. The social and economic situations of families and households vary as well as their degree of need or enterprise. The circumstances of forced migration entail at times traumatic separation and can be followed by upheaval in family organization.

A transnational family seeks ways to carry on with its core functions regardless of intervening geographic distance. These functions include caregiving, with particular focus on the young and elderly. Youth socialization lies in the realm of the family, as well as family welfare and wellbeing. This entails role shifts and adjustments. This is not always an easy task, since the outmigration of key members of the original family can leave gaps, which the non-mobile part of the family cannot fill adequately. It is not uncommon that the family members who migrate are those who might be better equipped to 'survive'. These might be the same individuals who held key responsibility roles for family welfare in the homeland. Income earning, caregiving and child/youth socialization resources are central factors in nuclear and extended family welfare and wellbeing.

Transnational migrants' remittances to the home country form a significant part of many sending countries' revenues. At the family level, remittances represent for many migrants the fulfilment of a role in income support for kin in the homeland, who in turn, undertake the caregiving and socialization activities of family members who have remained, or had to remain in the homeland. In this way transnational ties can feature strong reciprocity in intra-familial solidarity. Remittances can have a strong influence on socioeconomic coping of homeland kin. They can be decisive in helping a family out of absolute poverty. Remittances can also be seen as a type of informal social insurance, guaranteeing that it will be possible for the family to manage crises, and expenses incurred by sickness, care of the elderly, schooling, and repairs to dwellings, for example.

The sense of duty felt by migrants has sometimes a down-side when there is social pressure to remit. Settlement and integration into the labour markets can be a rocky path for migrants, especially in times of economic downturn in receiving countries. Attitudes and hiring become less generous toward newcomers. In more unfortunate cases, an unemployed migrant might not only be personally affected by an economically precarious position. Her or his relationship to close kin might also decline should the migrant feel stressed by social and family pressure or otherwise a sense of inadequacy in performing a responsibility role. This situation is complicated if communication becomes weaker in the process. There is a risk of this 'disconnection' of ties becoming interpreted as neglect, or lowered regard for family welfare. The inability to participate actively in family welfare generation could have a negative effect on a migrant's quality of settlement.

Zentgraf and Chinchilla (2012) state that parents who migrate without their children usually justify their migration decision on the grounds that the children and other family members, such as ageing parents, will be better off than if the migrating parent had remained. However in spite of the lack of proximity, migrant parents make ongoing efforts to keep up their parental roles and responsibilities in other ways which are possible over distance. Studies of transnational parenting practices give credit to migrant parents' strong and 'creative efforts to keep family members connected to and involved with each others' lives, even in the case of prolonged separation' (Zentgraf and Chinchilla, 2012, p.346). These authors state furthermore that engaging in transnational parenting practices is one way in which migrant parents can try to 'mitigate the cost of separation and tip the cost-benefit calculus in a positive direction'.

Countries with dynamic economies and labour needs encourage a migration pattern that involves the separation of parents and children. However transnational parenting is not without its many stresses and pitfalls. During the separation while parent/s settle, children are cared for, or fostered, by kin or close friends. These periods might be quite lengthy. Parents send remittance in money or in kind for the upkeep and care of their children. In her work on families of African Caribbean origin, Arnold's (2011) scrutiny is on parent-child relationships during family separation and reunion. Using an attachment theory framework, the author examines how separation from young children affects the quality of mother-child bonds and parent-child reunion processes which might prove to be traumatic or unsatisfactory. Arnold (2011) argues that broken attachments between young children and their mothers can lead to fractured mother-child relationships when reunited, to problems in developing trust in others as well as to later difficulties in forming strong attachments with partners and children in adulthood. Zentgraf and Chinchilla (2012) have drawn attention to the conscientious efforts of migrant parents to foster strong positive relationships over distance. Psychologists and other social service providers who work with reuniting families confirm that the quality of relationships during separation is a critical factor that influences the success of reunifications (Falicov, 2002).

The real costs of the migrant parent flows of today are not well known. The remittance flows to countries of origin have been viewed in a positive light. Remittances give families the opportunity to improve their socioeconomic conditions and can strengthen children's ongoing welfare and education. The social costs of parental migration to families and communities are difficult to estimate. Of concern is that migrating parents are probably only partially aware of the long term costs and benefits of family separation. The real costs and benefits of 'normalizing' family separation would need to be tracked longitudinally. When there is a stronger understanding of the dynamics of parental migration, it would be possible to develop local and national policies to reduce the social costs of family separation in the interests of positive reunification of families (Cortes, 2008; Zentgraf and Chinchilla, 2012).

Global Care Chains

The feminization of migration along with the growth of global care chains of today have fuelled parental migration and the inevitable family separation. Parrenas' (2000, p.561), the initial researcher on the trend of international careworking, states that:

> the migration and entrance into domestic work of Filipino women constitutes an international division of reproductive labor. This division of labor, which I name the international transfer of caretaking, refers to the three-tier transfer of reproductive labor among women in sending and receiving countries of

migration. While class-privileged women purchase the low-wage services of migrant Filipina domestic workers, migrant Filipina domestic workers simultaneously purchase the even lower-wage services of poorer women left behind in the Philippines. In other words, migrant Filipina domestic workers hire poorer women in the Philippines to perform the reproductive labor that they are performing for wealthier women in receiving nations.

Subsequently the term 'global care chain' was coined by Hochschild (2000) who theorized the phenomenon. Rush and Keenan (2014) comment that, at the heart of the matter, poor women from one part of the world care for the children of those who are better off, while in the homeland their own children are looked after by relatives or carers who are one economic rung below in the caring work hierarchy. Hassim (2008, p.397) observed that the ways and institutions through which unequal resources are distributed globally' are seen most clearly in the global care chain, and poses a most uncomfortable contemporary question, 'Can the gender-egalitarian model be achieved in rich countries without intensifying the global inequality in care provision?'

Many social phenomena have facilitated the marked growth in global care chains. The higher participation of women in the labour force of economically developed countries combined with inadequate public or other childcare services give rise to a demand for care workers. Workers are needed both for child care and for the care needs of the growing elderly population in economically developed countries. On the other hand, less economically developed countries hold a ready supply of potential workers to fill the caring deficits in other parts of the world. Women are predominant in the international caregiving sector. Easier and more affordable means of travelling and electronic communication help to bridge geographical distance. The growth of global care chains, the feminization of migration and restrictive family migration policies are key factors in family separation.

The Feminization of Migration

The independent out-migration of women has strengthened the income earning power in the family. Migrant careworkers often fill the role of the main breadwinner in transnational households. Domestic caregiving work is the main driver of international female labour migration. Scholars refer to this trend as the feminization of migration. There is a large body of research on this social shift in migration. Pantea (2012) looks at the surrogate parenting role of grandmothers in Romania. A large number of parents migrate for work. However the role of grandmothers has remained invisible and neglected in policies. The author asserts the need for cultural sensitive interventions aimed at increasing grandmothers' individual wellbeing. Attention is drawn also to the unresolved aspects of later life care needs of grandmothers themselves and traditional expectations for reciprocity. Boccagni (2014, p.236) looks at migrant careworkers' own care needs, pointing out that the latters' productive role remains also a reproductive one, and ' the transnational reach of this overlap makes it a still deeper source of tension, resentment and oppression'. Boccagni (2014) calls for the framing of institutional support for their cross-border caregiving, which should be a public responsibility at some level.

Chapter 8
Connectedness in an Interactive Systems Frame

Introduction

Many different modes of interaction with the receiving society are involved in immigrant integration. Their ability to make linkages in the society will be reflective of their participation, attachments and role efficacy in settlement. People find commonality in interest areas, work- and goal-focused cooperation, and in social relationships that can carry them into the life worlds of communities across the population. Initially family and kinship networks, or circles from their own ethnocultural background can create stability as individuals put down roots in the receiving society.

In this chapter, the main focus is on the types of instrumental interaction and participation modes that link social practitioners and settling actors and communities with formal and informal institutional spheres in settlement society. The institutional sphere is focused upon because this is generally the area with which settling groups have less strong connections. At the same time it is an area that can be influenced by social work. There is unlimited evidence to show that migrants themselves develop a rich range of social interaction modes as well as intercultural links in the informal areas. Structural or institutional integration is different since these are the sites of important opportunity areas which can in varying ways be sheltered or protected.

While much has been written about the value of immigrant participation across the society, less is generally known about the vertical positioning and status of minority members. The vertical integration of minorities and their access to positions and roles which cross boundaries into conventional established hierarchies will tell of equality in the society. Minority activists in Canada have emphasized the importance of immigrant representation across and at all levels of society, as one of the key indicators of integration. Social work and other professions working toward immigrant and social integration would need to focus also upon working *with* and *inside* institutions to transform systems toward more openness in admitting new groups as stakeholders, employees, service providers and actors at different levels in hierarchies.

The French concept of 'insertion' is useful here. The emphasis on 'insertion' and integration as appropriate responses to exclusion, featured in titles of social programmes which were introduced in France in, in the 1980s (Silver, 2007). For our purposes, insertion carries connotations of becoming positioned advantageously or strategically into existing areas or fields of action in settlement society. In a sense, it is more specific than the term integration. It evokes an idea which is not of coercion (as formerly was the case) but of decisively directing settlement interventions in order to facilitate immigrants' positioning in the society in such a way that there will be scope for their own integration initiatives and agency.

Integration means that an immigrant becomes part of society. It is a process of active connecting, featuring functional interdependence with different societal systems. Marginalization, separation and exclusion signify states of not-belonging, non-inclusion, and involuntary social peripheralization. I argue here that, as opposed to the idea of being socially disconnected in marginalization, *everyone is connected to the society in different ways*, with the connections being empowering or disempowering. From a purely binary perspective to facilitate clarity, the connections and configurations of connections through which individuals relate to the surrounding society can be seen as either positive or destructive of their wellbeing. Moreover these connections contribute differently to affect the course and quality of individuals' social settlement and integration into the receiving society.

Since individuals and groups do not live in a vacuum, the surrounding environment cannot be blotted out at will. To be a member of a negatively stereotyped group, for example, is to have to deal on an everyday basis with a very demanding type of externally imposed relationship with the surrounding human environment. To be subject to categorization as part of an ethnocultural group needing 're-socialization' as a condition for equal or the 'same' access as others to key social participation areas is an oppressing relationship. Being unemployed due to discrimination signifies being held in a societal relationship that continually displaces the individual. In this situation, activation policies and programmes that aim to prevent de-skilling and to sustain motivation and 'professional identity' are often a panacea, or a palliative measure. In the longer term, this surrogate type of connection to mainstream labour market has a counter-productive rather than a motivating effect if it promises to be the default alternative to societal integration. The settlement environment can take on characteristics of a liminal space in which it is difficult for societal rooting to take place.

The Frame of Connectedness in Interactive Systems

Immigrant integration can be conceptualized as 'connectedness', which in the positive sense has the potential of materializing in relationships to the society which promote membership and active participation on terms of fair treatment and equal respect. Recognition of the vital importance of constructive connections between immigrants and public fields of civic, economic and institutional activity is critical to the integration project. Social justice is reflected in positive connectedness with settlement society, which gives access to space for human agency. In one sense it is a question of a basic right to participate on a par alongside other nationals.

Social justice in society refers to the good of the whole community. This is taken to include both the good of each and the good of all, in an acknowledgement that one depends on the other.[1] Immigrant integration means inclusion of all groups into the sphere that is entitled to access and enjoy the common good, the good of each and the good of the whole, which are interdependent. Equality is one aspect of social justice. Equality 'can be measured by all people having equal access to, and participation in, a society's resources, institutions and conflict resolution mechanisms, with equal responsibility to shape and contribute to society' (Rudiger and Spencer, 2003, p.6).

Conceptualizing the Environment as an Action System

The social work focus on Person-In-Environment (PIE) is timeless and additionally it is adaptable to different contexts in time and place. For the integration context, PIE is well suited to charting the integration field and its dynamics comprehensively, and to engaging with presenting client situations in the context of societal conditions, systems and processes that impact integration (Bartlett, 1970). Integration and social work strategies alike purposefully target and work with systems in the settlement environment that hold key significance for immigrant insertion and integration.

I would like to propose here *a systems approach as a conceptual frame for 'connectedness' in immigrant integration.* Healy (2005, p.132) states that 'Systemic analyses focus on interactions within and across multiple 'social' systems, which can include the interpersonal system of family and friendship ties, neighbourhood system, organizational systems, social policy systems and social structural systems'. This author observes that systems perspectives have had significant influence on the formal base of social work. It is a frame that could inform social work practice and intervention modes in the integration field.

When institutions, groups, individuals, clients and citizens are conceptualized as systems, the inter-system connections are more than those between separate agents/players/actors. When systems rather than single actors interact, this will potentially affect in however small ways initially, whole systems rather than single

---

1 Available at: http://goo.gl/dZ1Hjt [Accessed 29 March 2015].

players. These constitute cross-system connections that also connect the entirety of these entities directly and indirectly because of the nature of a system's functioning, the close intra-system interrelationships and interdependence of its different parts and members. Thus the span of networking connections over systems is potentially greater than when separate or individual actors are connected.

It is proposed here that as a part of formal practice, targeting could be purposeful in order to identify and 'recruit' special contacts points or persons in any system, who would be amenable to join in to facilitate broader aims of immigrant integration into particular systems. These would constitute interactive chains of connections which practitioners and immigrants alike would foster and in which initiatives for inclusion and inclusionary goals could be advanced. These points, individuals or groups who are located in systems and strategically poised from the perspective of furthering integration aims, are themselves points of further connection and can be termed 'nodes', or linking individuals or groups. Being connected to those who have further connections is the start of wider connectedness. In this context it would be instrumentally focused connectedness. The proposed approach has affinity with networking, and 'snowballing' methods in fieldwork.

Cross systemic links can facilitate needed institutional change in at least two ways. Change can be a gradual symbiotic process arising out of interaction between actors and the consequent 'indirect' effects of this interaction. The results of interaction often can include increase in information, insight and understanding which possibly lead to evolution of ideas, perspectives, opinions and even shared convictions. Connections between systems can also feature conscious efforts to bring about change in either system.

One example would be a case of social workers who believe that family unification should be more broadly interpreted to include close relatives rather than being restricted to members of the immediate nuclear family. They are convinced that this would be a humane move to strengthen the support networks of newer citizens and also reinforce the resource base for more collective approaches to youth socialization in the family and community. The connection to a strategically situated 'actor system' in the responsible Ministry or Department could be developed as a conduit for advocacy, petition or information dissemination. Because of what is termed the 'reciprocity' feature of systems, the message or 'input' could be put through the system and work even gradually or incrementally toward 'change' internal to that system. In this manner, through more personal inter-node linking into other systems, it would be possible to complement and reinforce formal-type actions such as policy briefings, or direct political engagement.

System 'reciprocity' is an idea, based on internal dynamics in systems, that if one party of a system changes, the change interacts with all the other parts which therefore are also in the path of change (Payne, 1991, p.136). In other words, if a stimulus is introduced into a system (a government institution, for example), it will trigger a reaction in other parts of the system because of its patterns of interdependent parts in interrelationships. It is well known that in practice, to achieve change in institutional systems will invariably require repeated or multipronged stimuli. Much depends also on the positioning (or power) of the agent/actor in the targeted system. Possible change within the social worker system itself, which is the initiator node in the network of connectedness, might well be increased understanding of the context-related justifications for making a case for a more liberal family migration policy, or deeper insight into the policy dynamics in particular government ministries. Such activity could also be the springboard for close cooperation-based connectedness with immigrant clients and communities in change-focused activity to target institutions which are influential in shaping access policies in different social spheres.

An inherent characteristic of systems is the system boundary. Payne (1991, p.135) conceptualizes a system as 'an entity with boundaries within which physical and mental energy is exchanged more than it is across the boundary'. 'A closed system is where there is no interchange across the boundary' and 'an open system is where energy crosses the boundary which is permeable' (Payne, 1991, p.135).

When examining institutional boundaries, we know that these are more permeable to other institutions, but often closed to outsider change agents. Individuals from other similarly positioned and 'legitimate' institutions are more able to get through boundaries and to access decision-making and policy shaping levels. From a power perspective this can be understood as players of a certain status exercising 'position power' to gain access to other institutions. Social workers and others with position power or professional (expert) power would be in strategic positions to create networks of connectedness at this level. This would comprise the institutional level of inter-system connectedness which could be used to great advantage in promoting change in the interest of immigrant and social integration.

In Pierson's (2009, p.225) work on how social exclusion might be tackled, the author emphasizes that social workers' participation in building partnerships with other agencies is essential for addressing the complexity of social exclusion.

This system interaction has the potential of giving fuel to social and institutional change (depending on the nodes, and the quality of system interaction). It can constitute a type of continual indirect advocacy since there is much information and insight exchange as part of the interaction process, laying ground for stimulating ideas that could lead to 'action'. Moreover the opportunity to inform incremental change processes would be significant. Incremental changes at policy and institutional levels can be carried out in a context of a limited information base, or using 'bounded rationality', as explained in Chapter 4. To be connected into and contributing to incremental policy change processes would be a very important aspect of settlement and integration work.

Institutions, as systems, generally function in a 'steady state', and there are varying ways of receiving and using (or not using) input as they maintain themselves. To introduce 'change' into a system is to work toward a two way process of integration, with adaptation taking place also in the receiving systems of the society. Change agents need to draw on different sources of power when they initiate change strategies. They can employ power as *experts* in a certain area, as individuals or groups with particular *position* or status, and as persons with strategic *association* in vital areas – institutional, political, social, or client constituencies, for example.

A cooperative connectedness approach would have implications for power-sharing. Service users, who are immigrants in this case, gain recognition as experts on their own settlement conditions. Power derives from association with institutional insiders. Social work 'strength' or power is reinforced by closer association and collaboration with client and institutional systems. In one sense, professional power becomes allied with other kinds and sources of power. Alliance with different types of 'power' is likely to sharpen the emancipatory thrust of the profession.

Strategic interconnectedness is proposed here as an including mechanism. Systemic inter-institution connections represent only one type of connectedness at play in settlement. Immigrant community organizations which achieve standing in their communities can be connected with government institutions in mutually fruitful ways. Government institutions receiving solid inputs of grounded information can channel resources into organizational projects, and strengthen the wider mission of integration. Connectedness could embrace the transnational field where precedents already exist such as the codevelopment-focused cooperation in Spain that links the government, migrants and their organizations with development project organizers in countries of origin. At the national level, associations of immigrant professionals would have the potential to mobilize to advantage inclusive connections into the society-wide field of settlement and integration.

Immigrants as Persons in the Environment

The strength of connectedness of immigrants to the environment reflects the quality and level of their integration. Employment connections of individuals or groups could be occurring at levels below a glass ceiling in different sectors in the overall labour market system. Underemployed educated immigrants are among those with less than positive connectedness. From a systems perspective, when one immigrant or immigrant group gains entry to a specific workplace or employment system, it can introduce change in that the system might become more open to applicants with immigrant background. There is much evidence of this in the settlement experience and in the literature. Significantly when immigrants achieve positions in the hierarchical systems of employment or higher level education, for example, this can lower resistance barriers and bring changes for fair admission policies. This, in turn, will hold implications for productivity and added value in employing institutions, since the pool of candidates is not restricted.

The advantage of adopting a systems perspective is that it enables us to conceptualize a dynamic force in networking because introduction of change can spark a flow of change, however minimal at the outset. When agents as potential change agents are in contact, the initial stage of synergy creation is set. This cannot be expected as an automatic consequence of contacts, but in those interactive links between persons who discover commonality of ideas and purpose, there is much potential for spontaneous efforts to promote 'improvements' or change in systems. This style of action is grounded in systems, and driven by the initiatives of agents and groups purposively participating in many different contexts. It is a combination of small scale focused initiatives which can have cumulative influence in bringing about systemic responses to integration. Systemic adaptation and change can be viewed as an institutional parallel to the wide ongoing accommodation processes taking place on the ground in newer immigrant groups.

When it is possible to identify potentially positive outcomes of connectedness, efforts to build connectedness become meaningful to those who are involved in or committed to action in various capacities and fields. The systems perspective evokes the idea of synergy in interaction, since multiple types of interaction and connectedness lay a base for the collective pursuits of goals.

Systemic perspectives give a frame for holistic analysis, on the basis of which it would be possible to shape systemic interventions. Developing integration-facilitating connectedness to link change agents and immigrants widely with the environment and its institutions can be seen in itself as a systemic mechanism to counteract networked patterns of exclusion in societies. The argument is that discrimination in its various modes need not be an intractable social problem that is solely solved from the top down, or through legal proceedings. Boundaries between pro- and anti-integration attitudes are not set in stone, but should be seen as shifting and shiftable towards favouring more socially equitable positions. It would be possible to chart and mobilize systemic nodes favouring social justice solutions and to initiate systemic actions to counter-balance excluding forces in societies.

Affinities Across Diversity – Sharing Solidarities

Affinities and connectedness across diversity can give rise to solidarity of an enduring nature because these are founded on individuals' efforts to bridge difference in a productive way. We can hypothesize here that commonalities and affinities built across diversities are just as strong or might be stronger than those arising from 'categorical' uniformity that is the base of conventional anti-immigration opposition. Hierarchy cutting pathways of connectedness would be equality promoting. It is argued here that cross-cutting connectedness over boundaries (for example, through institutional boundaries or social hierarchies) can offset those reinforcing cleavage lines that are socially divisive (for example, when social marginality boundaries are superimposed along ethnic or class lines).

Connectedness can evolve into connections featuring solidarity. Solidarity towards the facilitation of integration would be based on acceptance of social justice principles, in the sense of a common good in which the good of each and the good of all are interwoven, with the one dependent on the other. A demonstrative willingness and commitment to cooperate to promote the common 'good' is implied. In addition to positive action, solidarity in this context also implies, in principle and practice (to the degree which it is possible), non-participation in and non-collusion with exclusionary efforts and projects which can be seen to diminish social justice and the principle of the common good.

Solidarity is seen here as very different from 'tolerance' which hardly binds people to the interests of fellow citizens. Tolerance can screen indifference or disengagement which exists alongside fiercely defended private interests or covertly exploitative relations. In the context of immigrant settlement, integration facilitating social relations hinge primarily on the generic principle of social justice, even while acknowledging that distributive issues or bundles of rights and entitlements are formal mechanisms of central importance. Integration is about newer citizens' ability to forge human pathways into the society and finding a meaningful place in it.

Xiberras (1993, p.196) observes that 'integration means solidarity, that is, the ability to re-establish mutual recognition by all parties in society. For the regulating State, this would mean the ability to handle the expression of a multitude of beliefs and values'.

Reducing the Bureaucentrism in Migrant Social Work

A concerted push to establish strong connections with the range of institutional, organizational and immigrant systems which have a participatory or possible participatory role in advancing social integration will be a shift away from the particular bureaucentric structures within which many of us must work. There is likely to be some diffusion, as opposed to concentration, of professional power as connections and connectedness evolve into cooperation. Through social work collaboration with their immigrant constituencies to shape, analyse and articulate their combined grounded knowledge of immigrant integration conditions, a unique and empowering information resource can be developed. It can be utilized in changing connections into socially transformative connectedness that reaches into public, civic, corporate and civil society systems. This would represent connectedness into decision-making systems. Likewise the forging of alliances and collaborative processes of connectedness with service user systems is one very effective way of combating undue bureaucentrism in social work.

Scrutiny of social work across various organizational and public contexts (from residual welfare systems to welfare states), suggests that rising bureaucentrism is a phenomenon closely but not exclusively tied to the elaboration of welfare systems. This seems to have been generally 'accepted' as an inevitable price of 'progress'. The open question on whether social work loyalty should be absolutely with the employing establishment is one facet of this. In any event, trying to compartmentalize loyalties, even professional ones, is to reduce the sophistication in institutional and societal relationships.

System Overlap

Some systems might work closely together and even partly overlap. Partial system overlapping is an interesting working mode, which can telescope the inter-systems distance. When systems can overlap, greater working synergy can be created, as for example, when immigrant community organizations have the mandate to share part of official service provision to settling communities and persons. Another example is when candidates from settling groups are trained and integrated into the majority social work cohorts. This is an obvious strategy to overcome language barriers and cultural gaps in the field, as well as being an egalitarian and more respectful approach when developing and delivering services to immigrant or minority communities.

The Operational Level

Inclusive systemic strategy aspects are proposed here as a way of counterbalancing institutional exclusiveness, and various excluding, non-permeable boundaries which arise in settlement situations. It should be recognized that some connections might remain latent for lengthy periods. Some systems might exhibit much lower levels of internal interdependence and interrelating. At one end of a systems continuum, systems might function purely as aggregates. At the other end they would be active and vibrant action systems. In order to bring the concept of system connectedness to the operational level, we can scrutinize the qualities of different types of connections. Social work models are very compatible with the theme of connectedness, and the principles and approaches highlighted here are used in practice. Connectedness is examined under four headings: functional, mode of operating, quality of interactiveness and outcomes.

- functional – purposeful or goal-focused in different areas, as in advocacy, education and information provision, research
- modes of operating – generalized exchange, brokering, reciprocal, altruistic, cooperative, collaborative
- quality of interactiveness – association, symbiotic links, affiliation, alliance, attachment, membership-type, partnership, interdependence, solidarity
- yields – inter-culturalism, empowerment, power, achievement of integration-facilitating goals, policy and programme validity, effectiveness and productivity, stronger understanding of presenting issues

Functional connections can be seen as purposeful in differing areas. The participants might cooperate around an outstanding issue or initiative that will contribute to an area of wellbeing in the society. Cooperation implies that individuals have a stake in the particular field or common pursuit. For newer citizens it can lead to 'belonging', even in the sense of national belonging, or belonging to a nation. Additionally contributing in the public sphere means participating in the arena of political life, from which participants can derive recognition and indeed, *power* of different types. This includes position power as an active and involved citizen which, in itself, can open spaces to new areas of agency. Advocacy is one of the central functions of social work with migrants. Beresford and Croft (2004) emphasize the importance of social work developing at this time, in collaboration with its service users, a central role for itself in public policy advocacy.

To be connected directly with individuals or groups representative of larger grouping or systems fosters a stronger understanding of the presenting issues, as compared with receiving information only through indirect channels. Moreover through association and communication there is, in general useful information exchange either purposefully or as a product of interaction. Interpersonal processes between the representatives of different groups can facilitate acculturation. Much of acculturation – understanding and adapting to another culture – takes place spontaneously through direct connection. Both immigrants and the receiving society become acculturated.

Systemic connectedness can furnish favourable channels for strategically targeted information dissemination, advocacy, expertise sharing, joint visioning and focused partnerships, generating social capital and not least fostering collaboration among stakeholder groups. Information sharing and channelling is to confront the problem of 'bounded rationality', when decision-makers make less than optimal choices based on the limited information they have at hand.

One of the most important areas of potential of system connectedness, and one of urgent contemporary significance, is in providing a forum for confrontational, adversarial or contentious discussion (see also Chapter 6). There is a glaring lack of this type of forum even in societies long experienced in immigration. Contention can be played out on the ground, sometimes with dire and violent consequences as we have witnessed in recent times. Should client systems and other issues-centred groups have a legitimate way to dialogue with those representatives of systems in which the conditions of integration are shaped, a valuable connecting space is created for feedback and input into the administrative and policy practices of integration. A 'legitimate' channel would be opened for the voice of settling groups – the other stakeholder system in integration and cultural diversification. Such opportunities for mutual exchange, discussion and critique, produce more unanimous solutions and ways forward because of a wide and authentic base of input from those concerned or affected.

System connectedness or overlap constitutes a tool to enable the identification and stemming of alienating processes in the society through preventive and proactive actions. Citizens' conventional societal connections to mainstream systems can be thin, not positive and even humiliating. In modern economically developed societies the periphery areas can be quite disconnected from the rest of society, with institutional systems inaccessible to marginalizing individuals and groups. Policy and academic research also produces material to inform policy. One of the issues is that research findings would call for being presented in policy friendly forms.

Connectedness in an Interactive Systems Frame

Figure 8.1 displays a chart of the field of possible paths of connectedness which could link immigrants and new citizens into societal institutions and social action systems. The quality and sturdiness of their linkages will determine how they will identify with settlement society and be disposed toward commitment to it. The threshold to contacts in civil society is traditionally low, since inclusivity is one of the features of its informal units of organization and institutions. Creating linkages to more formal-type institutions and action systems in the formal mainstream would need to be a joint undertaking of immigrants and social work, and members of majority society. It would be important for new citizens to be able to exercise agency also in the institutional sphere and in areas of public life which are generally the sites of tangible and intangible social resources.

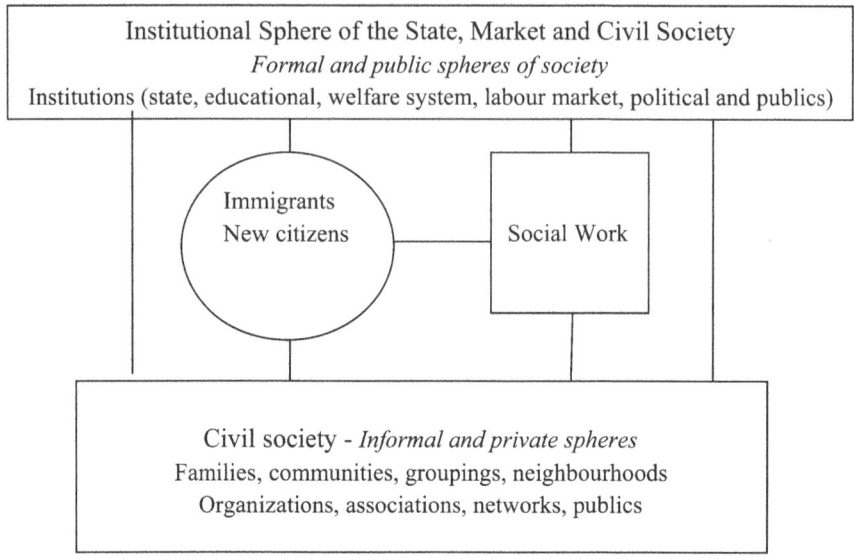

Figure 8.1   Interconnectedness in Interactive Systems

Connectedness would be a collective effort which could cumulatively have impact on the conditions in the settlement society, bringing needed changes and adjustments which would 'free' newer citizens from barriers to their productivity. Ultimately this works as an increase in the common good across the society.

Social Work Approaches and Connectedness

In the following, the different approaches to social work which are presented demonstrate that these all have affinity with aspects of a connectedness approach to social work with immigrants. Some of these models are very contemporary yet hinge strongly on generic principles and methods in the field.

The case management method of practice is the prime instrument of integration social work. Case management seeks to organize and coordinate a cluster of community services to meet the complex needs of clients in a manner that an individual service could not (Turner, 2005). Case management is especially relevant when clients' needs are intertwined. This style of practice depends on wide and effective social work networking with different service systems which specialize and target different service needs. As a central pillar of practice, case management methods can be used in all types of welfare systems and arrangements. It is difficult to imagine effective integration service responses without case management approaches.

Progressive social work reflects some of the central concerns in integration social work practice. Wright (2014, p.133) states that the progressive social work movement holds the conviction that many social issues, including poverty and unemployment, are not attributable to individual failure or choice but rather are structurally situated in the unequal distribution of power and resources. At the individual level progressive social work supports the efforts of those in oppressing circumstances to combat their alienation and sense of powerlessness by gaining more control over their own lives and social conditions.

Practitioners working from a progressive social work perspective shift their emphasis from expert knowledge and distributive formula for institutional resources to working professionally 'in collaboration with the clients, where power differentials are explicitly recognized and the clients are supported to produce a range of options' that will bring improvements in their life situations (Wright, 2014, p.135; Campbell and Ungar, 2003).

Progressive social work is carried out also at the structural level, using various methods including advocacy and user involvement in order to effect policy change and bring about more socially just systems (Mullaly, 2002).

Harington and Beddoe (2014) argue for a more robust civic profession in New Zealand and elsewhere. They encourage the profession to engage in policy roles, stressing that an informed and articulate profession will be able to argue against flawed policy. The authors draw attention to the fact that practitioner-led research which is presented in a scholarly manner is a powerful tool that can be advantageous in advocacy and efforts focused on service improvement (Beddoe and Harington, 2012).

Being at the front lines and knowing the stories behind cases, civic social workers 'might invite users and communities to contribute to an understanding about *what isn't working*' (Harington and Beddoe, 2014, p.159). In civic social work practice, 'knowledge is co-constructed in partnership with community, individuals, families and with co-workers. The value of knowledge gained at the front line is that it is should be shared' (Harington and Beddoe, 2014, p.159).

Inclusive social work practice (ISWP) has significant affinity with the idea of connectedness that is proposed here. Strier's (2013) model is based on the four methodological principles of involvement, partnership, advocacy, and conscientization. These respond to the main features of social exclusion which are extreme social isolation, growing dependency, multiple deprivation, and internalized oppression. The model is explained below with a focus on practitioner – client/community relationships. However the principles are readily operationalized along the whole matrix of interconnecting relations proposed here, and bring constructive elements to functional connections.

Involvement can be manifested by the social worker at emotional, moral, intellectual and behavioural levels. At the emotional level, the social worker makes an emotional investment in the process of building a personal relationship with the community members. Moral involvement with excluded communities calls for taking a definite moral stand against exclusion, or identifying morally with the cause and suffering of the client.

Intellectual involvement requires the participant to be informed. The complexity of the social exclusion phenomenon calls for 'understanding of its specific foundations and dynamics' (Strier, 2013, p.348). Behavioural involvement relates to intensity of commitment. Strier (2013, p.348) states 'Against the background of social isolation, involved, inclusive practice should display a high level of intensity, able to trigger action, to ignite the hearts and to illuminate the minds, to inspire a sense of hope'.

Strier (2013, p.348) makes the contrast between dependency which 'means unequal, asymmetrical, and sometimes paternalistic relations' and partnership which means 'creating a relationship based on equality, mutual respect, joint activity, and joint learning'.

Advocacy aims at helping marginalized communities in the voicing of their claims and concerns and in the carrying out of effective strategies to fight their social exclusion. Strier (2013) comments that in the light of the prevalence of socially excluding phenomena, the ISWP conceptual framework proposes that social services professionals should take on advocacy roles as an essential, rather than marginal, part of their practice on behalf of their clients.

Conscientization or consciousness-raising is a critical part of ISWP. The conscientization concept of Freire (1972) proposes a way for excluded communities to achieve a deeper understanding of their social world. This would put them on the path toward reshaping their future. Conscientization progresses in the context of egalitarian dialogue, in which social workers, family and community members participate in collective reflection on social issues which have a significant effect on their wellbeing. Participants analyse the assumptions they have held about the social world and build new ways of seeing and relating to it. Participants begin to see themselves as agents and historical subjects who are able to take possession of their own history. Strier (2013) calls for reshaping of traditional social work principles to confront the challenges of growing social exclusion phenomena in modern societies.

Chapter 9
Shaping Our Future Community

In this final chapter I set out a number of areas and issues which I consider would need to be revisited and addressed in policy strategy and practice contexts. These have been discussed in the text but are pulled together here more concisely. These are arranged under the headings: policy and strategy, social work practice, practice environments and social work education.

Policy and Strategy

Policy Processes and Communities

Calls for political and public policymakers to engage seriously with their immigrant communities, groupings and representatives have come from many migration researchers based in different disciplines and societies (Beresford and Croft, 2004; Faulkner, 2010; McNeil, 2012; Townsend, 1970; Wieviorka, 2011). Immigrants need to be part of the 'solution' to integration challenges. This entails their inclusion in integration-related policy dialogues, in strategy formulation and implementation. Effective and democratic approaches to the societal processes in integration should include newer citizens in roles of subjects in policy and research activity.

Settling groups and individuals can contribute unique grounded insights into the aetiology of problems and the feasibility of service, programme and policy approaches which target their own groups. Information of this kind can serve to reduce the level of 'risk' when policy shifts or changes are being shaped. Moreover, in addition to contributing sociocultural expertise, they would be in a position to mobilize a wider support base for programme initiatives through their social and 'symbolic' capital in the particular groupings. When community representatives from immigrant organizations, religious and interest groups take part in policy processes, the legitimacy base is strengthened. This is a critical aspect in demanding or innovative interventions which may be very well received in communities, provided that these can be seen to be serving the 'common good'. Once political and public policymakers engage seriously with immigrant representatives in their common interests for developing a shared community, a vital level of the integration process is ushered in, with the promise of numerous downstream positive effects.

Focused interventions can be carried out proactively from a developmental perspective. The course and outcomes of integration are of high concern to immigrants and the whole 'immigrant community' who are often aware of emergent problems and crises well before these actually surface. Proactive approaches would need to be given priority. In this activity, the settling communities and individuals themselves are key stakeholders and actors. Many members of immigrant communities are dedicated to working toward productive and positive outcomes of incorporation. Using its outreach and community development methods for keeping near to its clients and service users, social work would be in a strong strategic position for proactive initiatives.

Anti-exclusion

A critical issue for policy focus is the response to contemporary social exclusion phenomena. Socioeconomic exclusion has repercussions in all areas of social life, and the way we shape responses will have high significance for social integration in economically developed receiving societies. Inequality in institutional policies and hiring practices in public and private sector employment, imposes a positive and affirmative duty on authorities. The methods of combating discrimination are known and available. The establishment of independent public equality bodies with power of investigation is key to anti-discrimination. This type of mandate would in itself have weight from the outset in the fight against discrimination.

Promotion of equal access can also take the form of positive promotion of good practice in the public and private sectors (Rudiger and Spencer, 2003, p.22). Such initiatives would be one facet of a wider effort to mainstream integration goals across different sectors and institutions.

Families and Socialization

We are familiar with the saying that it takes a village to bring up a child in traditional societies. It can be argued that the social environment in 'modern' societies and communities also play a critical role in socializing youth because there is regular interface and interaction. The proactive and continuing effort to fight negative and racist stereotyping in the living environment can be justified also on the grounds of its importance to youth socialization processes. Families generally provide supportive environments and try to foster protective factors which serve to buffer hostility or antagonism that might be experienced.

Racism can be personally internalized by individuals who experience it. It can undermine individuals' self-perception and self-esteem, especially if it not counteracted by supportive and protective mechanisms. Negative relations with the surrounding society can take a course toward social alienation. Young people growing up in an environment with racism should be focused upon for special support programmes that would complement intra-familial and other support sources. It would be important for the society itself to reach out by formally acknowledging the existence of the problem. An unconditional social investment is called for to combat negative effects on youth and to keep them in mainstream participatory sectors.

Social Work Practice

Family-oriented Approaches

Social work with immigrants would often call for family-oriented methods. These take into account the circumstances of many migrant families who are in the process of gradually re-establishing their social and close networks of interaction and mutual support. The family is the core and sometimes sole support system of its members. It follows that fragility of family relations or distress arising out of adapation transitions would call for responses that directly or indirectly seek to affirm and reinforce family roles and strengths. Social work has a wide range of approaches, methods, frames and concepts which are suited for application in the context of families as well as individuals.

Family group conferencing enhances the agency of family members for resolving problem situations collectively and 'democratically'. The strengths perspective can entail exploration and discovery of unique resources of strengths and resilience which migrants bring with them. These in turn can be adapted to underpin settlement processes.

Clear understanding of the parenting styles of the cultures from which migrants come will be critical for practitioners. On the other hand, understanding of the parenting style in the new society will be crucial for immigrant parents, since they will need to be able to synthesize differing cultural practices in order to guide their children on the two planes of cultural adaptation and socialization. Family social work would involve parental support in both endeavours in the new society.

Cohering Cultures

Practitioners' keen awareness of their own cultural background would help them to draw the limit on what degree of cultural adaptation might be expected of new groups. Knowledge of one's culture against the backdrop of a world of cultures will make for a balanced non-universalizing perspective on one's own culture. Cultures are sources of meaning, values, beliefs and strengths which have helped people to 'survive' and 'thrive'. Multiculturalism assumes that there is social and societal space for all of these and that space will be made for them.

Case Management

Case management is a mode of generalist social work that offers a unique holistic approach to settlement and integration work. The method has particular affinity with the scope of integration activities and the field of individuals' efforts in settlement. The case management process involves charting of the areas for attention and/or intervention, jointly with immigrant service users.

Case management can be used in a time dimension frame to project the sequence and profile of expected integration outcomes, including the lesser, as well as the more significant, all of which contribute to the composite effort. In this way, immigrant clients might gain a sharper outlook on future stages of settlement. Additionally it may be of help in identifying more efficient or direct paths to participation in the mainstream. This would need to be a democratic exercise that respects immigrant service-users' autonomy as well as personal aspirations which are the driving force in settlement.

The Migrant Social Work Relationship

The social worker interaction with families and individuals who are new to the receiving society is distinctive. Initially the practitioner-service user relation will be one in which immigrant clients have some of their first impressions of the human face of institutions in the receiving society. This is one of the particular facets of social work with newcomer clients, and it keeps us aware of how and what we represent establishment-wise and society-wise. It is in one sense the reverse side of the PIE coin, in which we are the Practitioners in [Social and Institutional] Environment!

Practice Environments

Welfare Systems

Social work is carried out in or in association with different types of welfare systems – from the residual and fragmented at one end of a continuum, to the well-resourced and tightly organized at the other. There is large diversity in how welfare systems are organized. Every system has its 'strengths', 'weaknesses' as well as particular characteristics arising out of the social context. These will affect practice modes, but not the quality of practice, which is based on universal elements intrinsic to the profession.

In residual systems, practitioners need to be anchored in a very purposeful way to the fundamental principles and values of the profession, since the work is organized in a more fluid institutional and possibly fluctuating environmental context. The mission must constantly be in the range of focus, and a guide and a support. With respect to resources, these can be thin. For example, income support eligibility could be very restricted (such as to mother's with young children but not the 'able bodied' who are seen as being able work regardless of whether there are job opportunities or not). The benefits and services might not be sufficient for families to escape out of chronic poverty.

Developed welfare states are relatively very well resourced and better organized. Moreover, as Ahmed-Mohammed (2013, p.464) observes, since social work is carried out on a base of institutional power in public bodies which are strongly legitimized by society to promote general welfare, practitioners are ethically grounded without needing to question their everyday professional practice. This can be argued to be positive and emancipating for practice. Alternatively fundamental principles and values can be crowded out by bureaucentric routines and categories, necessitating on the part of practitioners, constant alertness to keep above the bureaucratic level. Bureaucracy, however, is also present in residual systems. In the developed welfare state the benefit and service response is more 'generous'. The central challenge in migrant integration is to ensure that these actually match presenting integration needs of service users.

Professional teams in migrant social work need to include minority social workers. The integration of the workplace can be promoted by practitioners themselves and through Human Resource channels.

Leading and Leadership

Social work in the integration field needs effective leadership with the knowledge, skills, ideals and vision which will do justice to the profession and its singular potential. Suitable individuals for leadership would, in addition to possessing administrative skills, also have knowledge of migration and integration, as well as the societal dynamics of settlement. Leadership quality is generally a critical element of the practice environment. It will be decisive in determining whether the potential of migrant social work practice is developed and realized. This has wide-reaching implications for wellbeing in the immigrant community, and for the national immigrant integration programme as a whole.

Political, resource and municipal-level factors in the course of policy implementation often bring about a policy dilution process. The spirit and original intent of the policy might become blurred on the way towards the implementation stage. Policy interpretation and its application modes need to be guided by informed, insightful and sometimes courageous decisions.

Social Work Education

Some of the areas which would be valuable in social work education for the immigrant integration field are discussed in this section in the following order: practicum placements, training for leadership and continuing education, learning from other countries.

Practicum is usually very significant in a student's period of study. Good placements open an exciting window onto the field and draw students into the heart of practice. Since social work with migrants is a relativity new area, supervision capacity might sometimes be stretched. An alternative would be mixed placement arrangements that would allow a student to gain experience in direct practice and also in fields of activity related to settlement, for example, immigration, housing, education, health, and the labour market. This would be justified by the practitioner's need for insight into processes and dynamics in the social and institutional environment. It would also furnish a base for future networking.

Formal social work education of today would need to include component/s on how social work is conducted in other societies in order to offset tendencies toward a nation-centric outlook. For example, African countries are faced with large scale refugee flows which often remain in protection/exile for long periods. Social work with migrants is carried in all countries with migrant populations and where social work is established. There are stocks of new knowledge on settlement and integration and on social work practice in different locations. It would be advantageous to be familiar with welfare arrangements in the societies of origin from which migrants in the newer South-North flows originate.

In order to address the need for representation of minority social work professionals in the field of settlement and integration, it would be necessary to start at the level of training and education of suitable individuals. This would be the case,in particular, in new gateway societies, where immigration is relatively new.

Workers from ethnocultural communities often have precarious positions in integration services although they bring special skills and knowledge, which are a valuable resource in cross-cultural services. Barberis and Boccagni (2014, p.i80) state that the role of specialist 'intercultural mediators has suffered from weak institutionalisation' as well as lack of national standards, precarious working contracts, and limited recognition within professional teams'. Walsh, Este and Krieg (2008) also draw attention to the key roles of community workers with linguistic and culturally relevant skills who should be engaged in employment and service provision. This aspect of fragility in settlement service provision would be addressed through Human Resource intervention and not least, through education and training programmes which would lead to formalization of the role and position of individuals specialized in intercultural relations.

Research

While the body of social work research on migration and settlement is growing, researchers send a clear message that there are several important gaps. The lack of rich qualitative data on the perspectives of social service users and recipients across the social and human services can lead to government reliance on number crunching to guide policy processes. Users' and practitioners' experiences and serious critique from the field are muted in policymaking and evaluation, and replaced by mechanical statistical exercises and compliance reports (Faulkner, 2010; Harington and Beddoe, 2014; Scheyett, 2006; Townsend, 1970).

The danger exists that 'the subjects of research (namely, people from vulnerable culturally diverse communities) become marginalized in the knowledge production process because of their low social power as stakeholders in the welfare state' (Clarke, 2009, p.23). Compounding this situation is the fact that migrants' low power is often hardly a reflection of their educational levels since these can be very poorly measured.[1] Clarke (2009, p.23) argues that 'debate on the preconditions necessary to create diverse narratives on knowledge production could be an important step forward towards developing more transformative and inclusive social work research in Finland and elsewhere'.

The condition of underemployment of immigrants, which is implied above, is often discussed in studies. However research on the scale of this problem in receiving societies is scant even though the problem has been widely observed and of contemporary importance. Without more precise and grounded information on immigrant underemployment it is difficult to make a case for it to be addressed. Qualitative and quantitative data would tell of different important aspects such as the proportion of the immigrant population that is affected, the nature of the gap between education levels and actual employment, the aetiology of career loss, the scale of outward employment-motivated emigration (as well as involuntary staying-in-place) of educated migrants, long-term economic effects on social security, as well as consequences for family wellbeing. Immigrant underemployment has economic, social and political implications for settlement societies, since it signifies a continuing leakage of human capital and a condition that undermines the time, resources and energies which are invested in social integration. It is also a question of how seriously equality principles are regarded in the polity.

The functional outcomes of integration have generally been the focus of studies which highlight, for example, areas of education, employment, housing and health (Korac, 2003). There is need for greater research focus on the process of integration, as well as on how institutions are adapting or would

---

1　See Pekkala (2005).

need to adapt to respond to new needs that newcomers may have' (Phillimore, 2008, p.322).

Longitudinal data, including qualitative data, would tell of the patterns of intergenerational incorporation and provide insight into whether or not formal settlement and integration approaches and policies have been effective. Second generation marginalization and disaffiliation is a current concern in receiving societies.

Cox and Geisen (2014) state that there is an urgent need for 'larger numbers of comparative international social work studies, seeking more nuanced understandings of social relations, social conditions and social differences between countries'. The authors point out that such comparative studies would provide opportunities for international dialogue and contribute to developing internationally grounded knowledge on the topic of migration.

McNeil (2012, p.103) brings out the policy function of social research, stating that 'Publicizing research and advocacy efforts is just as important as doing them'. Since the thrust of much of social research is toward institutional or social change, the findings of studies would need to be presented in versions accessible to policymakers, political decision-making bodies, administrators and the public.

Social work practice with migrants draws on the rich range of skills, methods, and values of generic social work. Since social work has come to occupy a central role in immigrant settlement and integration, it is time to consolidate models and composite approaches to this particular area of practice. Due to the variation in and within migrant populations, and the different practice contexts, alternative practice approaches would be needed. Practice approaches or models would combine or synthesize skills and approaches suitable to a range of presenting tasks, settlement contingencies and challenges. These would offer alternative guides to working in context-responsive ways with our different client constituencies.

The particular strengths of migrants have not often been focused upon in studies. This area would generate ideal opportunities for practitioner-immigrant research. Additionally collaboration on this topic could have far-reaching empowering outcomes. The migrant experience is far more than the immediate cultural encounter. It resonates with resilience building and coping processes common to the human condition in every society.

A Long View

Social work continues to mediate some of the most critical linkages between social, economic and political spheres in the pursuit of ideals which are rooted in the common good. Its potential field of engagement encompasses the whole society. There is, at the same time, opportunity to discover, include and activate human, social and civil resources at all levels.

Social work is indeed a fascinating profession. It knits together what can be termed 'altruistic' elements with extremely practical aspects in order to shape responses to client situations in a holistic approach which can be offered by no other profession. The skill required for keeping a fine balance between these two core elements of practice runs deep through the entire portfolio of approaches, methods and interventions.

Bibliography

Agoumy, T. and Tamim, M., 2009. Migration, Networks and Territories in the Ouneine Valley, High Atlas, Morocco. *Journal of Ethnic and Migration Studies*, 35(10), 1679–97.

Ahmed-Mohamed, K., 2013. Pragmatism and Interest: Immobilism of Social Work in the Welfare State. *International Social Work*, 56(4), 455–66.

Alba R.D., 1990. *Ethnic Identity: The Transformation of White America*. New Haven, CT: Yale University Press.

Alba, R. and Nee, V., 1997. Rethinking Assimilation Theory for a New Era of Immigration. *International Migration Review*, 31(4), 826–74.

Alghasi, S., Eriksen, T.H. and Ghorashi, H. eds, 2009. *Paradoxes of Cultural Recognition: Perspectives from Northern Europe*. Farnham: Ashgate Publishing.

Arnold, E., 2011. *Working with Families of African Caribbean Origin: Understanding Issues around Immigration and Attachment*. London and Philadelphia, PA: Jessica Kingsley Publishers.

Banton, M., 1987. *Racial Theories*. Cambridge: Cambridge University Press.

Barberis, E. and Boccagni, P., 2014. Blurred Rights, Local Practices: Social Work and Immigration in Italy. *British Journal of Social Work*, 44, s1, pp.i70-i87.

Barnes, D., 2001. Resettled Refugees' Attachment to their Original and Subsequent Homelands: Long-term Vietnamese Refugees in Australia. *Journal of Refugee Studies*, 14(4), 394–411.

Barnetz, Z. and Vardi, S., 2014. Moving Ahead, Falling Apart, Losing Power: Three Narratives to the Development of Human Services. *Journal of Progressive Human Services*, 25(2), 75–97.

Bartlett, H., 1970. *The Common Base of Social Work Practice*. Washington: National Association of Social Workers.

Beck, U., 2000. *What is Globalization?* Cambridge: Polity Press.

Beddoe, L., 2011. Investing in the Future: Social Workers Talk about Research. *British Journal of Social Work*, 41(3), 557–75.

Beddoe, L. and Harington, P., 2012. One Step in a Thousand-mile Journey: Can Civic Practice be Nurtured in Practitioner Research? Reporting on an Innovative Project. *British Journal of Social Work*, 42(1), 74–93.

Beitz, C.R. and Goodin R.E., 2009. Introduction: Basic Rights and Beyond, in *Global Basic Rights*, edited by C.R. Beitz and R.E. Goodin. Oxford: Oxford University Press, pp.1–24.

Beresford, P. and Croft, S., 2004. Service Users and Practitioners Re-united: The Key Component for Social Work Reform. *British Journal of Social Work*, 34(1), 53–68.

Berg, M.L. and Eckstein, S., 2013. Re-Imagining Migrant Generations. *Journal of Ethnic and Migration Studies*. Special Issue Introduction.

Berry, J.W., Kalin, R. and Taylor, D.M., 1977. *Multiculturalism and Ethnic Attitudes in Canada*. Ottawa: Minister of Supply and Services.

Betts, A., 2013. *Survival Migration: Failed Governance and the Crisis of Displacement*. New York: Cornell University Press.

Betts, A., 2009. *Forced Migration and Global Politics*. Chicester: John Wiley & Sons.

Biles, J., Carroll, A., Pavlova, R. and Sokol, M., 2012. Canada – Fostering an Integrated Society?, in *International Perspectives: Integration and Inclusion*, edited by J. Frideres and J. Biles. Montreal and Kingston: McGill-Queen's University Press, pp.79–110.

Bisley, N., 2007. *Rethinking Globalization*. Basingstoke: Palgrave Macmillan.

Boccagni, P., 2012. Practising Motherhood at a Distance: Retention and Loss in Ecuadorian Transnational Families. *Journal of Ethnic and Migration Studies*, 38(2), 261–77.

Bolzman, C., 2012. Democratization of Ageing: Also a Reality for Elderly Immigrants?, *European Journal of Social Work*, 15(1), 97–113.

Bolzonaro, F., 2010. The Uncertain Destiny of an Incomplete Revolution. *Work, Employment and Society*, 24(3), 591–6.

Boswell, C., 2007. Theorizing Migration Policy: Is There a Third Way? *International Migration Review*, 41(1), 75–100.

Brown, S.K. and Bean, F.D., 2006. *Assimilation Models, Old and New: Explaining a Long-Term Process*. Migration Information Source, Migration Policy Institute.

Bryceson, D. and Vuorela, U., eds. 2002. *The Transnational Family: New European Frontiers and Global Networks*. New York: Berg.

Bukasa, P.K., 2010. Transnational Family Ties, Remittance Motives, and Social Death among Congolese Migrants: A Socio-Anthropological Analysis. *Journal of Comparative Family Studies*, 41(2), 225–43.

Butler, J., 2008. A Response to Ali, Beckford, Bhatt, Modood and Woodhead. *British Journal of Sociology*, 59(2), 255–60.

Calhoun, C., 1999. Nationalism, Political Community and the Representation of Society Or, Why Feeling at Home is not a Substitute for Public Space. *European Journal of Social Theory*, 2(2), 217–31.

Campbell, C. and Ungar, M., 2003. Deconstructing Knowledge Claims. *Journal of Progressive Human Services*, 14(1), 41–59.

Caponio, T., 2010. Conclusion: Making Sense of Local Migration Policy Arenas, in *The Local Dimensions of Migration Policymaking*, edited by T. Caponio and M. Borkert. Amsterdam: Amsterdam University Press, pp.161–95.

Carruthers, A., 2013. National Multiculturalism, Transnational Identities. *Journal of Intercultural Studies*, 34(2), 214–28.

Castel, R., 2000. The Roads to Disaffiliation: Insecure Work and Vulnerable Relationships. *International Journal of Urban and Regional Research*, 24(3), 519–35.

Castles, S., 2013. The Forces Driving Global Migration. *Journal of Intercultural Studies*, 34(2), 122–40.

Castles, S., 2004. Why Migration Policies Fail. *Ethnic and Racial Studies*, 27(2), 205–27.

Castles, S., 2003. Towards a Sociology of Forced Migration and Social Transformation. *Sociology*, 37(1), 13–34.

Castles, S. and Davidson, A., 2000. *Citizenship and Migration: Globalization and the Politics of Belonging*. London: Macmillan.

Cetrez, Ö.A., 2005. *Meaning-Making Variations in Acculturation and Ritualization: A Multi-generational Study of Suroyo Migrants in Sweden*. Department of Theology: Uppsala University.

Chambers, N. and Canesan, S., 2005. Refugees in Canada, in *Cross Cultural Caring: A Handbook for Health Professionals*, 2nd edn, edited by N. Waxler-Morrison, J. Anderson, E. Richardson, and N. Chambers. Vancouver, BC: University of British Columbia Press, pp.289–322.

Chaskin, R.J., Brown, P., Venkatesh, S. and Vidal A., 2001. *Building Community Capacity*. New York: Aldine De Gruyter.

Chesters, G. and Welsh, I., 2011. *Social Movements: The Key Concepts*. NY: Routledge.

Clarke, K., 2009. Negotiating Migrant Community Needs through Social Work Research A Finnish Example. *Qualitative Social Work*, 10(1), 8–27.

Clegg, S., Kornberger, M. and Pitsis, T, 2008. *Managing and Organizations: An Introduction to Theory and Practice*. Los Angeles: Sage Publications.

Coffey, A., 2004. *Reconceptualizing Social Policy: Sociological Perspectives on Contemporary Social Policy*. Berkshire: Open University Press.

Cohen, R., 1997. *Global Diasporas: An Introduction*. Seattle, WA: University of Washington Press.

Coleman, J.S., 1988). Social Capital in the Creation of Human Capital. *The American Journal of Sociology*, 94, 95–120.

Colombo, A. and Sciortino, G., 2004. Italian Immigration: The Origins, Nature and Evolution of Italy's Migratory Systems. *Journal of Modern Italian Studies*, 9, 49–70.

Cortes, R., 2008. Children and Women Left Behind in Labour Sending Countries: An Appraisal of Social Risks. New York: UNICEF.

Cortes, D.E., 1995. Variations in Familism in Two Generations of Puerto Ricans. *Hispanic Journal of Behavioral Sciences*, 17, 249–55.

Cox, P. and Geisen, T., 2014. Migration Perspectives in Social Work Research: Local, National and International Contexts. *British Journal of Social Work*, 44, pp.i157-i173.

Craig, G., 2002. Poverty, Social Work and Social Justice. *British Journal of Social Work*, 32(6), 669–82.

Crisp, J., 2003. Refugees and the Global Politics of Asylum. *The Political Quarterly*, 74, Issue Supplement s1, pps. 75–87.

Danso, R., 2009. Emancipating and Empowering De-Valued Skilled Immigrants: What Hope does Anti-Oppressive Social Work Practice Offer? *British Journal of Social Work,* 39(3), 539–55.

de Beer, P. and Koster, F., 2009. *Sticking Together or Falling Apart: Solidarity in an Era of Individualization and Globalization.* Amsterdam: Amsterdam University Press.

Delanty, G., 2009. *The Cosmopolitan Imagination: The Renewal of Critical Social Theory.* Cambridge: Cambridge University Press.

Dilley, R., 2010. Reflections on Knowledge Practices and the Problem of Ignorance. *Journal of the Royal Anthropological Institute,* 16(1) (N.S.), S176-S192.

Dodgsen, J. and Struthers, R., 2005. Indigenous Women's Voices: Marginalization and Health. *Journal of Transcultural Nursing,* 16(4), 339–46.

Dorais, L-J., 2009. The Vietnamese in Montreal, Canada: Reflections on Intangible Capital and Immigration. *Asian and Pacific Migration Journal,* 18(2), 231–54.

Duffy, B., 2014. Perceptions and Reality: Ten Things We Should Know About Attitudes to Immigration in the UK. *The Political Quarterly*, 85(3), 259–66.

Duneier, M., 1992. *Slim's Table: Race, Respectability, and Masculinity.* Chicago and London: University of Chicago Press.

Dunn, K., 2010. Guest Editorial. Embodied Transnationalism: Bodies in Transnational Spaces. *Population, Space and Place,* 16, 1–9.

Dunn, K.M., 2005. A Paradigm of Transnationalism for Migration Studies. *New Zealand Population Review*, 31, 15–31.

Eastmond, M., 2011. Egalitarian Ambitions, Constructions of Difference: The Paradoxes of Refugee Integration in Sweden. *Journal of Ethnic and Migration Studies*, 37(2), 277–95.

Engebrigtsen, A., 2007. Kinship, Gender and Adaptation Processes in Exile: The Case of Tamil and Somali Families in Norway. *Journal of Ethnic and Migration Studies*, 33(5), 727–46.

Erdal, M.B. and Oeppen, C., 2013. Migrant Balancing Acts: Understanding the Interactions Between Integration and Transnationalism. *Journal of Ethnic and Migration Studies*, 39(6), 867–84.

Ernst, R., 2010. *The Price of Progressive Politics: The Welfare Rights Movement in an Era of Color Blind Racism.* New York: New York University Press.

Evans, T. and Harris, J., 2004. Street-Level Bureaucracy, Social Work and the (Exaggerated) Death of Discretion. *British Journal of Social Work*, 34(6), 871–95.

Faas, D., 2010. *Negotiating Political Identities: Multiethnic Schools and Youth in Europe*. Farnham: Ashgate Publishing.

Falicov, C.J., 2002. Ambiguous Loss: Risk and Resilience in Latino Immigrant Families, in *Latinos: Remaking America*, edited by M. Suárez-Orozco. Berkeley, CA: University of California Press, pp.274–88.

Faulkner, A., 2010. *Changing Our Worlds: Examples of User-Controlled Research in Action*, Eastleigh, INVOLVE.

Favell A., 2014. The Fourth Freedom: Theories of Migration and Mobilities in 'Neo-liberal' Europe. *European Journal of Social Theory*, 17(3), 275–89.

Favell, A., 1998. *Philosophies of Integration: Immigration and the Ideal of Citizenship in France and Britain*. Basingstoke: Macmillan.

Ferguson, B.R., 1996. Integration and the Vietnamese Community in Australia. *Integration*, 4(11), 64–7.

Finch, J.F., Okun, M.A., Pool, G.J. and Ruehlman, L.S., 1999. A Comparison of the Influence of Conflictual and Supportive Social Interactions on Psychological Distress. *Journal of Personality*, 67(4), 581–621.

Fontes, L., 2002. Child Discipline and Physical Abuse of Immigrant Latino Families: Reducing Violence and Misunderstandings. *Journal of Counseling and Development*, 80(1), 31–40.

Forsander, A. and Alitolppa-Niitamo, A., 2000. *Employment of Immigrants and Labour Administration in Finland*. Helsinki: Tyohallinnon julkaisu 242.

Fraser, N., 1987. *Social Movements vs. Disciplinary Bureaucracies: The Discourse of Social Needs*. CHS Occasional Paper No. 8. Center for Humanistic Studies. Minneapolis, MN: University of Minnesota.

Fraser, N., 1994. After the Family Wage: Gender Equity and the Welfare State. *Political Theory*, 22(4), 591–618.

Freeman, G.P., 2004. Immigrant Incorporation in Western Democracies. *International Migration Review*, 38(3), 945–69.

Freeman, G.P., 1986. Migration and the Political Economy of the Welfare State. *The Annals of the American Academy of Political and Social Science*, 485 (May), 51–63.

Freire, P., 1972. *Pedagogy of the Oppressed*. London: Penguin Books.

Frye, M., 1983. *The Politics of Reality: Essays in Feminist Theory*. Trumansburg, NY: Crossings Press.

Fyvie, A., Ager, A., Curley, G. and Korac, M., 2003. *Integration Mapping the Field Volume II: Distilling Policy Lessons from the 'Mapping the Field' Exercise*. UK Home Office. Available at: http://webarchive.nationalarchives.gov.uk/20110218135832/rds.homeoffice.gov.uk/rds/pdfs2/rdsolr2903.pdf [Accessed: 2 April 2015].

Gabaccia, D.R., 2006. *Today's Immigration Policy Debates: Do We Need a Little History?* Migration Policy Institute (MPI November 1, 2006, Feature. http:// www.migrationpolicy.org/article/todays-immigration-policy-debates-do-we-need-little-history [Accessed 20 April 2015].

Ghorashi, H., 2007. *Why Ayaan Hirsi Ali is Wrong. Halleh Ghorashi argues only openness to migrants' decisions can help steer clear of cultural fundamentalism.* Available at: http://www.signandsight.com/features/1250.html [Accessed: 20 April 2015].

Ghorashi, H., Eriksen, T.H. and Alghasi, S., 2009. Introduction, in *Paradoxes of Cultural Recognition: Perspectives from Northern Europe*, edited by S. Alghasi, T. Hylland Eriksen and H. Ghorashi. Farnham: Ashgate Publishing, pp.1–15.

Giddens, A., 1990. *The Consequences of Modernity.* Cambridge: Polity Press.

Glick-Schiller, N., Basch, L. and Szanton-Blanc, C., 1992. *Towards a Transnational Perspective on Migration: Race, Class, Ethnicity, and Nationalism Reconsidered.* New York: New York Academy of Sciences.

Glick-Schiller, N., Basch, L. and Szanton-Blanc, C., 1995. From Immigrant to Transmigrant: Theorizing Transnational Migration. *Anthropological Quarterly*, 68(1), 48–63.

Gordon, M.M., 1964. *Assimilation in American Life: The Role of Race, Religion, and National Origins.* New York: Oxford University Press.

Granovetter, M.S., 1973. The Strength of Weak Ties. *American Journal of Sociology*, 78(6), 1360–81.

Guild, E., Groenendijk, K. and Carrera, S. eds, 2009. *Illiberal Liberal States: Immigration, Citizenship and Integration in the EU.* Farnham: Ashgate Publishing.

Gullestad, M., 2002. Invisible Fences: Egalitarianism, Nationalism and Racism. *Journal of the Royal Anthropological Institute*, 8(1), 45–63.

Hall, E.T., 1976. *Beyond Culture.* Garden City, NY: Anchor Press/Doubleday.

Handelman, D., 1976. Bureaucratic Transactions: The Development of Official Client Relationships in Israel, in *Transaction and Meaning. Directions in the Anthropology of Exchange and Symbolic Behaviour*, edited by B. Kapferer. Philadelphia, PA: Institute for the Study of Human Issues, pp.223–75.

Harington, P.R.J. and Beddoe, L., 2014. Civic Practice: A New Professional Paradigm for Social Work. *Journal of Social Work*, 14(2), 147–64.

Harwood, R.L., Schoelmerich, A., Ventura-Cook, E., Schulze, P.A., and Wilson, S.P., 1996. Culture and Class Influences on Anglo and Puerto Rican Mothers' Beliefs Regarding Long-term Socialization Goals and Child Behavior. *Child Development*, 67, 2446–61.

Hassim, S., 2008. Global Constraints in Gender Equality in Care Work. *Politics and Society*, 36(3), 388–402.

Healy, K., 2005. *Social Theories in Context: Creating Frameworks for Practice.* Basingstoke: Palgrave Macmillan.

Herberg, D.C., 1993. *Frameworks for Cultural and Racial Cultural Diversity.* Toronto: Canadian Scholars Press.

Higham, J., 1984. *Send These to Me: Immigrants in Urban America.* Revised Edition. Baltimore and London: The Johns Hopkins University Press.

Hochschild, A.R., 2000. Global Care Chains and Emotional Surplus Value, in *On The Edge: Living with Global Capitalism,* edited by W. Hutton and A. Giddens. London: Jonathan Cape, pp.130–46.

Hoefer, R., 2010. Introduction: Contemporary Research on Social Work Advocacy and Policy Practice. *Journal of Policy Practice,* 9(3/4), 161–3.

Hollifield, J., 2004. The Emerging Migration State. *International Migration Review,* 38, 885–912.

Hugo, G., 2013. *What we know about Circular Migration and Enhanced Mobility.* Policy Brief No 7. Migration Policy Institute.

Hughes, P., 1999. Recognizing Substantive Equality as a Foundational Constitutional Principle. 22 *Dalhousie Law Journal* L.J.5.

Heckmann, F., 2007. *Towards a Better Understanding of Human Smuggling.* IMISCOE Policy Brief No. 5, November 2007.

Inglis, C., 1996. *Multiculturalism: New Policy Responses to Diversity.* Management of Social Transformations (MOST) – UNESCO. Available at: http://www.unesco.org/most/pp4.htm [Accessed 20 April 2015].

Iosifides, T. and Lavrentiadou, M., Petracou, E. and Kontis, A., 2007. Forms of Social Capital and the Incorporation of Albanian Immigrants in Greece. *Journal of Ethnic and Migration Studies,* 33(8), 1343–61.

Islamic Council of New South Wales 2004. *Challenges for Australian Muslims: Discrimination, Anti-Terrorism, and the Media.* Chullora: Islamic Council of New South Wales.

Jansson, B.S., 2003. *Becoming an Effective Policy Advocate: From Policy Practice to Social Justice.* Pacific Grove, CA: Brooks/Cole/Thomson Learning.

Kallen, E., 1995. *Ethnicity and Human Rights in Canada.* Toronto: Oxford University Press.

Kasinitz, .P, Mollenkopf, J.H. and Waters M.C, eds, 2004. *Becoming New Yorkers: Ethnographies of the New Second Generation.* New York: Russell Sage Foundation.

Kastoryano, R., 2000. Settlement, Transnational Communities and Citizenship. *International Social Science Journal,* 52, 307–12.

Kaufman, E., 2014. 'It's the Demography, Stupid': Ethnic Change and Opposition to Immigration. *The Political Quarterly,* 85(3), 267–76.

Kilkey, M. and Merla, L., 2014. Situating Transnational Families' Care-giving Arrangements: The Role of Institutional Contexts. *Global Networks,* 14(2), 210–47.

Kirby, L.D. and Fraser, M., 1997. Risk and Resilience in Childhood, in *Risk and Resilience in Childhood: An Ecological Perspective,* edited by M. Fraser. Washington, DC: NASW Press.

Kivisto, P., 2003. Social Spaces, Transnational Immigrant Communities, and the Politics of Incorporation. *Ethnicities*, 3(1), 5–28.

Kivisto, P. and Wahlbeck, O., 2013. *Debating Multiculturalism in the Nordic Welfare States*. Basingstoke: Palgrave Macmillan.

Kivisto, P. and Wahlbeck, Ö., 2013. Debating Multiculturalism in the Nordic Welfare States, in *Debating Multiculturalism in the Nordic Welfare States*, edited by P. Kivisto and Ö. Wahlbeck. Basingstoke: Palgrave Macmillan, pp.1–21.

Kivisto, P., 2001. Theorizing Transnational Immigration: A Critical Review of Current Efforts. *Ethnic and Racial Studies*, 24(4), 549–77.

Klocker, N. and Dunn, K.M., 2003. Who's Driving the Asylum Debate? Newspaper and Government Representations of Asylum Seekers. *Media International Australia*, 109, 71–92.

Kofman, E., 2004. Family-related Migration: A Critical Review of European Studies. *Journal of Ethnic and Migration Studies*, 30(2), 243–62.

Korac, M., 2003. Integration and How We Facilitate It: A Comparative Study of the Settlement Experiences of Refugees in Italy and the Netherlands. *Sociology*, 37(1), 51–68.

Kottak, C., 2005. *Window on Humanity: A Concise Introduction to Anthropology*. 2nd edn. Boston, MA: McGraw-Hill.

Lacroix, T., 2013. Collective Remittances and Integration: North African and North Indian Comparative Perspectives. *Journal of Ethnic and Migration Studies*, 39(6), 1019–35.

Lacroix, T., 2009. Transnationalism and Development: The Example of Moroccan Migrant Networks. *Journal of Ethnic and Migration Studies*, 35(10), 1665–78.

Lazarus, R.S. and Folkman, S., 1984. *Stress Appraisal and Coping*. New York: Springer.

Law, L., 2003. Transnational Cyberpublics: New Political Spaces for Labour Migrants in Asia. *Ethnic and Racial Studies*, 26(2), 234–52.

Levine, P., 2011. What Do We Know about Civic Engagement? *Liberal Education*, 97(2), 12–19.

Lewin, K., 1946. Action Research and Minority Problems. *Journal of Social Issues*, 2(4), 34–46. Available at: http://infed.org/mobi/kurt-lewin-groups-experiential-learning-and-action-research [Accessed 20 April 2015].

Lewis, D., 2002. Civil Society in African Contexts: Reflections on the Usefulness of a Concept. *Development and Change*, 33(4), 569–86.

Lindblom, C.E., 1959. The Science of 'Muddling Through'. *Public Administration Review*, 19, 79–88.

Lloyd, J., 2003. The Closing of the European Gates? The New Populist Parties of Europe. *The Political Quarterly*, 74, Issue Supplement s1, pp.88–99.

Loeb, P.R., 2010. *Soul of a Citizen: Living with Conviction in Challenging Times*. New York: St. Martin's Press.

Long, K. and Crisp, J., 2010. Migration, Mobility and Solutions: An Evolving Perspective. *Forced Migration Review*, 35, 56–7.

Lorenz, W., 2006. *Perspectives on European Social Work: From the Birth of the Nation State to the Impact of Globalisation*. Opladen: Barbara Budrich.

Lundy, C. and van Wormer, K., 2007. Social and Economic Justice, Human Rights and Peace: The Challenge for Social Work in Canada and the USA. *International Social Work*, 50(6), 727–39.

Luthar, S.S. ed., 2003. *Resilience and Vulnerability: Adaptation in the Context of Childhood Adversities*. Cambridge: Cambridge University Press.

Lyons, K., Manion, K, and Carlsen, M., 2006. *International Perspectives on Social Work: Global Conditions and Local Practice*. Basingstoke: Palgrave Macmillan.

Mann, A., 1979. *The One and the Many: Reflections on the American Identity*. Chicago, IL: Chicago University Press.

March, J.G. and Simon, H.A., 1993. *Organizations*. 2nd Ed. Wiley-Blackwell.

Maslow, A.H., 1943. A Theory of Human Motivation. *Psychological Review*, 50(4), 370–96.

McConnell, S., 2004. Advocacy in Organizations: The Elements of Success. *Generations*, 28, 25–30.

McNeil, L. ed., 2012. *Street Practice: Changing the Lens on Poverty and Public Assistance*. Farnham: Ashgate Publishing.

Mehdi, A., 2004. Globalization, Migration and the Arab World, in IOM, 2004. *Arab Migration in a Globalized World*. IOM, Geneva, pp.11–19.

Melucci, A., 1989. *Nomad of the Present*. Philadephia, PA: Temple University Press.

Mernissi, F., 2000. *The New Cheherazads: Women and Civil Society in Digital Islam 2* Booklet 2000. Text for her word-image exhibition and workshop project at the American University, 15–16 April 2000.

Modood, T., 2003. Muslims and the Politics of Difference. *The Political Quarterly*, 74, Issue Supplement s1, pp.100–15.

Mogro-Wilson, C., 2013. Parenting in Puerto Rican Families. *Families in Society*, 94(4), 235–41.

Mogro-Wilson, C., 2008. The Influence of Parental Warmth and Control on Latino Adolescent Alcohol Use. *Hispanic Journal of Behavioral Sciences*, 30(1), 89–105.

Mogro-Wilson, C., 2011. Resilience in Vulnerable and At Risk Latino Families. *Infants and Young Children*, 24(3), 267–79.

Moussa, A., 2004. *Arab Migration in a Globalized World*. IOM, Geneva. Acknowledgements pp.7–8.

Mullaly, B., 1997. *Structural Social Work: Ideology, Theory and Practice*. Oxford: Oxford University Press.

Mullaly, B., 2002. *Challenging Oppression: A Critical Social Work Approach*. Oxford: Oxford University Press.

Munz, R., 2013. Demography and Migration: An Outlook for the 21st Century. Migration Policy Institute (MPI). Policy Brief No. 4. Available at: http://www.migrationpolicy.org/research/demography-and-migration-outlook-21st-century [Accessed 20.4.2015].

Murphy, L.B., 2000. *Moral Demands in Nonideal Theory*. Oxford: Oxford University Press.

Nagel, C.R. and Staeheli, L.A., 2008. Integration and the Negotiation of 'Here', and 'There': The Case of British Arab Activists. *Social & Cultural Geography*, 9(4), 415–30.

Newland, K., Agunias, D.R. and Terrazas, A., 2008. *Learning by Doing: Experiences of Circular Migration*. Insight: Program on Migrants, Migration, and Development. Migration Policy Institute.

Nicholson-Crotty, J., 2007. Politics, Policy and the Motivations for Advocacy in Nonprofit Reproductive Health/Family Planning Providers. *Nonprofit and Voluntary Sector Quarterly*, 36, 5–21.

Nussbaum, M.C., 1999. Women and Equality: The Capabilities Approach. *International Labor Review*, 138(3), 227–51.

O'Brien, M., 2011. Equality and Fairness: Linking Social Justice and Social Work Practice. *Journal of Social Work*, 11(2), 143–58.

Olwig, K.F., 2011. 'Integration': Migrants and Refugees between Scandinavian Welfare Societies and Family Relations. *Journal of Ethnic and Migration Studies*, 37(2), 179–96.

Ostergaard-Nielsen, E., 2011. Codevelopment and Citizenship: The Nexus Between Policies on Local Migrant Incorporation and Migrant Transnational Practices in Spain. *Ethnic and Racial Studies*, 34(1), 20–39.

Pantea M-C., 2012. Grandmothers as Main Caregivers in the Context of Parental Migration. *European Journal of Social Work*, 15(1), 63–80.

Papademetriou, D., 2003. Managing Rapid and Deep Change in the Newest Age of Migration. *The Political Quarterly*, 74, Issue Supplement s1, pps. 39–58.

Parekh, B., 2010. What is Multiculturalism?, in *The Ethnicity Reader: Nationalism, Multiculturalism and Migration*, edited by M. Gubernau and J. Rex. 2nd ed. Cambridge: Polity Press, pp.238–50.

Parrenas, R., 2000. Migrant Filipina Domestic Workers and the International Division of Reproductive Labor. *Gender and Society*, 14(4), 560–80.

Payne, M., 1991. *Modern Social Work Theory: A Critical Introduction*. Basingstoke: The Macmillan Press.

Pekkala, S., 2005. *Increasing Labour Supply through Economic Migration*. Government Institute for Economic Research. Finland 23–24 June 2005. Available at: http://www.mutual-learning-employment.net/pdf/05_irland/FI_Pekkala.pdf. [Accessed 20 April 2015].

Penninx, R., 2003. Integration: The Role of Communities, Institutions, and the State. *Migration Information Source*, Special Issue (October): Integration

& Immigrants. Washington: Migration Policy Institute. Available at: http://www.migrationpolicy.org/print/4810#.VE4a0ctMtjo [Accessed 27 October 2014].

Perlmann, J. and Waldinger, R., 1997. Second Generation Decline? Children of Immigrants, Past and Present-A Reconsideration. *International Migration Review*, 31(4), Special Issue: Immigrant Adaptation and Native-Born Responses in the Making of Americans, pp.893–922.

Phillimore, J. and Goodson, L., 2008. Making a Place in the Global City: The Relevance of Indicators of Integration. *Journal of Refugee Studies*, 21(3), 305–25.

Phillips, A., 2007. *Multiculturalism Without Culture*. Princeton, NJ: Princeton University Press.

Phillips, R. ed., 2009. *Muslim Spaces of Hope: Geographies of Possibilities in Britain and the West*. London: Zed Books.

Pierik, R., 2004. Conceptualizing Cultural Groups and Cultural Difference: The Social Mechanism Approach. *Ethnicities*, 4(4), 523–44.

Pitkanen, P. and Satu Kouki., Meeting Foreign Cultures: A Survey of the Attitudes of Finnish Authorities Towards Immigrants and Immigration. *Journal of Ethnic and Migration Studies*, 28(1), 103–18.

Portes, A., 2003. Conclusion: Theoretical Convergences and Empirical Evidence in the Study of Immigrant Transnationalism. *International Migration Review*, 37(3), 874–92.

Portes, A., Guarnizo, L.E. and Landholt, P., 1999. The Study of Transnationalism: Pitfalls and Promise of an Emergent Research Field. *Ethnic and Racial Studies*, 22(2), 217–37.

Portes, A. and Rumbaut, R.G., 2001. *Legacies: The Story of the Immigrant Second Generation*. New York: Russell Sage Foundation.

Portes, A. and Zhou, M., 1993. The New Second Generation: Segmented Assimilation and Its Variants. *Annals of the American Academy of Political and Social Sciences*, 530, 74–96.

Potocky, M., 2010. The Travesty of Human Trafficking: A Decade of Failed U.S. Policy. *Social Work*, 55(4), 373–5.

Prandini, R., 2014. Family Relations as Social Capital. *Journal of Comparative Family Studies*, 45(2), 221–34.

Prandini, R., 2007. Il capitale sociale familiare in prospettiva relazionale: come definirlo, misurarlo e sussidiarlo. *Sociologia e Politiche Sociali*, 10(1).

Ramadan, T., 2012. *Islam and the Arab Awakening*. New York: Oxford University Press.

Reid, E.J., 2000. Understanding the Word 'Advocacy': Context and Use, in *Structuring the Inquiry into Advocacy*, edited by E.J. Reid. Washington, DC: Urban Institute, pp.1–7.

Rodgers, O.W., 2013. *Beginnings, Middles, & Ends, Sideways Stories on the Art and Soul of Social Work*. Harrisburg, PA: White Hat Communications.

Rome, S.H., Hoechstetter, S. and Wolf-Branigin, M., 2010. Empowering Clients for Political Action. *Journal of Policy Practice*, 9(3/4), 201–19.

Rönnqvist, S., 2009. Strategies from Below: Vietnamese Refugees, Education, Secondary Moves and Ethnic Network, in *Resettled and Included: The Employment Integration of Resettled Refugees in Sweden*, edited by P. Bevelander, M. Hagström and S. Rönnqvist. Malmö: Malmö Institute for Studies of Migration, Diversity and Welfare.

Rudiger, A. and Spencer, S., 2003. *Social Integration of Migrants and Ethnic Minorities: Policies to Combat Discrimination*. Brussels: The European Commission and the OECD.

Rush, M. and Keenan, M., 2014. The Social Politics of Social Work: Anti-Oppressive Social Work Dilemmas in Twenty-First-Century Welfare Regimes. *British Journal of Social Work*, 44(6), 1436–53.

Saggar, S., 2003. Immigration and the Politics of Public Opinion. *The Political Quarterly*, 74, Issue Supplement s1, pp.178–94.

Said, E.W. 1978 *Orientalism*. New York: Random House.

Sayad, A., 1999. *The Suffering of the Immigrant* (preface by Pierre Bourdieu). Cambridge: Polity Press.

Scheyett, A., 2006. Silence and Surveillance: Mental Illness, Evidence-based Practice, and a Foucualtian Lens. *Journal of Progressive Human Sciences*, 17(10), 71–92.

Scholten, P., 2011. *Framing Immigrant Integration: Dutch Research-Policy Dialogues in Comparative Perspective*. Amsterdam: Amsterdam University Press.

Sen, A., 1999. *Development as Freedom*. Oxford: Oxford University Press.

Shenhav, Y., 1999. *Manufacturing Rationality: The Engineering Foundations of the Managerial Revolution*. Oxford: Oxford University Press.

Shue, H., 1996. *Basic Rights: Subsistence, Affluence, and US Foreign Policy*. 2nd ed. Princeton, NJ: Princeton University Press.

Silver H., 2007. *Social Exclusion: Comparative Analysis of Europe and Middle East Youth*. Middle East Youth Initiative Working Paper, Wolfensohn Center For Development Dubai School of Government.

Silver, H. and Miller, S.M., 2006. From Poverty to Social Exclusion: Lessons from Europe, in *The Emerging Agenda: Poverty and Race in America*, edited by C. Hartman. Lanham, MD: Lexington Books, pp.57–70.

Silver, H., 1994. Social Exclusion and Social Solidarity: Three Paradigms. *International Labour Review*, 133(5–6), 531–7.

Silvermint, D., 2013. Resistance and Wellbeing (Resisting One's Oppression), *The Journal of Political Philosophy*, 21(4), 405–25.

Skey M., 2014. 'How Do You Think I Feel? It's My Country': Belonging, Entitlement and the Politics of Immigration. *The Political Quarterly*, 85(3), 326–32.

Smith, M.P., 2007. The Two Faces of Transnational Citizenship. *Ethnic and Racial Studies*, 30(6), 1096–116.

Smith, A.D., 1994. The Problem of National Identity: Ancient, Medieval and Modern? *Ethnic and Racial Studies*, 17(3), 375–99.

Smith, M.P. and Guarnizo, L.E. eds, 1998. *Transnationalism From Below*. New Brunswick: Transaction Publishers.

Smith, R.C., 2003. Diasporic Memberships in Historical Perspective: Comparative Insights from the Mexican, Italian and Polish Cases. *International Migration Review*, 37(3), 724–59.

Spencer, S., 2003a. *The Challenges of Integration for the EU*. October 1, 2003. Available at: http://www.migrationpolicy.org/print/4808#.VE5IYhY9uTM. Accessed 26 October 2014.

Stolcke, V., 1995. Talking Culture. New Boundaries, New Rhetorics of Exclusion in Europe. *Current Anthropology*, 36(1), 1–13.

Strier, R., 2013. Responding to the Global Economic Crisis: Inclusive Social Work Practice. *Social Work*, 58(4), 344–53.

Snyder, C.R. ed., 1999. *Coping: The Psychology of What Works*. Oxford: Oxford University Press.

Sydow, J. and Koch, J., 2009. Organizational Path Dependence: Opening the Black Box. *Academy of Management Review*, 34(4), 689–709.

Taylor, C. 1992. *Multiculturalism and the Politics of Recognition: An Essay*. Princeton: Princeton University Press.

Thompson, N., 1998. *Promoting Equality: Challenging Discrimination and Oppression in the Human Services*. New York: Macmillan.

Thomas-Hope, E.M., 1999. Return Migration to Jamaica and its Development Potential. *International Migration*, 37(1), 183–207.

Thomas-Hope, E., 2009. Cultures of Freedom and Constraint in Caribbean Migration and Diaspora, in *Freedom and Constraint in Caribbean Migration and Diaspora*. edited by E. Thomas-Hope. Kingston and Miami: Ian Randle Publishers, pp.xxv-xlvi.

Tilly, C., 1998. *Durable Inequality*. Berkeley, CA: University of California Press.

Townsend, P. ed., 1970. *The Fifth Social Service: A Critical Analysis of the Seebohm Proposals*. London: The Fabian Society.

Triandafyllidou, A., 2010. Irregular Migration in Europe in the Early 21st Century, in *Irregular Migration in the European Union: Evidence, Facts and Myths*, edited by A. Triandafyllidou and D. Vogel. Aldershot: Ashgate, pp.1–21.

Tuori, S., 2007. Cooking Nation: Gender Equality and Multiculturalism as Nation-Building Discourses. *European Journal of Women's Studies February*, 14(1), 21–35.

Turner, F.J., 2005. *Encyclopedia of Canadian Social Work*. Waterloo: Wilfred Laurier University Press.

Turton, D., 2003. *Conceptualising Forced Migration*. RSC Working Paper No. 12. Refugee Studies Centre, University of Oxford.

Turton, D. and Marsden, P., 2002. Taking Refugees for a Ride? The Politics of Refugee Return to Afghanistan. Afghan Research and Evaluation Unit, Kabul and Islamabad.

Ungar, S., 2008. Ignorance as an Under-identified Social Problem. *The British Journal of Sociology*, 59(2), 301–26.

Ungar, M., 2008. Resilience across Cultures. *British Journal of Social Work*, 38(2), 218–35.

UNESCO, 2014. *Migration and Inclusive Societies*. Available at http://www.unesco.org/new/en/social-and-human-sciences/themes/international-migration [Accessed 20 April 2015].

United Nations, 2000a. *Protocol against the Smuggling of Migrants by Land, Air and Sea, supplementing the United Nations Convention against Transnational Organized Crime*. New York: United Nations Publications.

United Nations, 2000b. *Protocol to Prevent, Suppress and Punish Trafficking in Persons, Especially Women and Children*, adopted by the United Nations General Assembly Resolution 55/25 of 14 November 2000, supplementing the UN Convention against Transnational Organized Crime.

UNRISD, 1994. *Social Integration: Approaches and Issues*. UNRISD Briefing Paper No. 1. World Summit for Social Development. March 1994.

Valtonen K., 1994. The Adaptation of Vietnamese Refugees in Finland. *Journal of Refugee Studies*, 7(1), 63–78.

Valtonen, K.,1998. Resettlement of Middle Eastern Refugees in Finland: The Elusiveness of Integration. *Journal of Refugee Studies*, 11(1), 38–60.

van Hear, N., 1998 *New Diasporas: The Mass Exodus, Dispersal and Regrouping of Migrant Communities*. London: UCL Press.

Van Soest, D., 2012. Confronting Our Fears and Finding Hope in Difficult Times: Social Work as a Force for Social Justice. *Journal of Progressive Human Services*, 23(2), 95–109.

Vogel, D. and Triandafyllidou, A., 2005. *Civic Activation of Immigrants – An Introduction to Conceptual and Theoretical Issues*. Interdisciplinary Center for Education and Communication in Migration Processes (IBKM) University of Oldenburg. POLITIS – Working Paper No.1.

Wahlbeck, O., 2002. The Concept of Diaspora as an Analytical Tool in the Study of Refugee Communities. *Journal of Ethnic and Migration Studies*, 28(2), 221–38.

Wahlbeck, O., 2004. Turkish Immigrant Entrepreneurs in Finland: Local Embeddedness and Transnational Ties, in *Transnational Spaces*, edited by M. Povrzanovic Frykman. Malmö: Malmö University Press, pp.101–22.

Wahlbeck, Ö. 2015. The Finnish and Swedish Migration Dynamics and Transnational Social Spaces. *Mobilities*, 10(1), 100–18.

Wahlbeck, Ö. and Olsson, E., 2007. Diaspora – ett berest begrepp, in E. Olsson, C. Lundqvist, A. Rabo, L. Sawyer, Ö. Wahlbeck, and L. Åkesson, *Transnationella rum*. Umeå: Boréa.

Waldinger, R. and Fitzgerald, D., 2004. Transnationalism in Question. *American Journal of Sociology*, 109(5), 1177–95.

Walsh, C.A., Este, D. and Krieg, B., 2008. The Enculturation Experience of Roma Refugees: A Canadian Perspective. *British Journal of Social Work*, 38(5), 900–17.

Walzer, M., 2015. Islamism and the left. *Dissent*, 62(1), 107–17.

Waters, M.C. and Jimenez, T.R., 2005. Assessing Immigrant Assimilation: New Empirical and Theoretical Challenges, *Annual Review of Sociology*, 31, 105–25.

Waters, M., 1990. *Ethnic Options: Choosing Identities in America*. Berkeley, CA: University of California Press.

Waters, J., 2003. Flexible Citizens? Transnationalism and Citizenship in Amongst Economic Immigrants in Vacnouver. *The Canadian Geographer*, 47(3), 219–34.

Wieviorka, M., 1998. Is Multiculturalism the Solution? *Ethnic and Racial Studies*, 21(5), 881–919.

Wieviorka, M., 2011. A World in Movement. *Migraciones Internacionales*, 6(1), 45–60.

Prodita Sabarini, 2011. Michel Wieviorka: Discussing Multiculturalism. *The Jakarta Post*. Wednesday March 23 2011. Available at: http://www.thejakartapost.com/news/2011/03/23/michel-wieviorka-discussing-multiculturalism.html-0#sthash.CsbohZcP.nHMTg8uz.dpuf [Accessed 20.4.2015].

Wieviorka, M., 2014. *The End of Multiculturalism*. Presentation at ISA World Congress of Sociology, Yokohama, July 2014.

Wilson, W.J., 1987. *The Truly Disadvantaged The Inner City, the Underclass, and Public Policy*. Chicago, IL: University of Chicago Press.

Wimmer A. and Glick-Schiller, N., 2002. Methodological Nationalism and Beyond: Nation-state Building, Migration and the Social Sciences. *Global Networks*, 2(4), 301–34.

Wright, K.N., 2014. The Practical Realities of Implementing Progressive Social Work: A Case Example in Parenting Education. *Journal of Progressive Human Services*, 25(2), 133–53.

Wu, Q., Tsang, B. and Ming, H., 2014. Social Capital, Family Support, Resilience and Educational Outcomes of Chinese Migrant Children. *British Journal of Social Work*, 44(3), 636–56.

Xiberras, M., 1993. *Les theories de l'exclusion*. Paris: Meridiens Klincksieck.

Xie, Y. and Greenman, E., 2005. *Segmented Assimilation Theory: A Reformulation and Empirical Test*. Population Studies Center Research Report 05-581, Population Studies Center, University of Michigan, Institute of Social Research.

Young, I.M., 1990. *Justice and the Politics of Difference*. Princeton, NJ: Princeton University Press.

Young, I.M., 2004. Responsibility and Global Labor Justice. *The Journal of Political Philosophy*, 12(4), 365–88.

Zentgraf, K.M. and Chinchilla, N.S., 2012. Transnational Family Separation: A Framework for Analysis. *Journal of Ethnic and Migration Studies*, 38(2), 345–66.

Zhou, M., 1997a. Segmented Assimilation: Issues, Controversies, and Recent Research on the New Second Generation. *International Migration Review*, 31(4), Special Issue: Immigrant Adaptation and Native-Born Responses in the Making of Americans, pp.975–1008.

Zhou, M., 1997b. Growing Up American: The Challenge Confronting Immigrant Children and Children of Immigrants. *Annual Review of Sociology*, 23,.63–95.

Žižek, S., 2008. *Violence: Six Sideways Reflections*. London: Profile Books.

Index